ASSAULT ON LAKE CASITAS

Books by Brad Alan Lewis

Wanted: Rowing Coach – a semi-fictional story of my coaching the UCSB rowing team.

Lido for Time: 14:39 – my training journal from 1983-84, with elaborations, insights, and an exceptional waffle recipe.

Walking Towards Thunder – a great book about hiking the John Muir Trail.

The Last Car in the Parking Lot – an even better book about hiking the John Muir Trail.

(and several other books I have disowned.)

ALSO THE DOCUMENTARY

A Fine Balance, about the making of the US men's Olympic 8+ from the 2000 Sydney Olympic Games, available on DVD from JL Racing, 1-800-831-3305.

For photo captions, many more photos and contact information, visit: www.bradalanlewis.com

ASSAULT ON LAKE CASITAS

BRAD ALAN LEWIS

SHARK PRESS

2011

Assault on Lake Casitas by Brad Alan Lewis
All rights reserved, copyright 1990

ISBN - 13: 978-14609-144-58
ISBN - 10: 14-609-144-57

Second printing: 2002
Third printing: 2007
Fourth printing: 2009
Fifth printing: 2011

Acknowledgements: Scott Zimmer, Chris Clark, Dan Louis, Paula Oberstein. Your encouragement through all the years was invaluable. Now, finally, let's go surfing. Gabriella Goldstein - without you this book would never have been possible. Carl Hilterbrand, the best teacher of toughness in the world. Duvall Hecht - many years ago, you lent me the use of your cherished Pocock single scull, the *By George*. For the first time, I was able to enjoy the pleasure of gliding over an unbroken pool of water in a delicate racing scull. The feeling, the rhythm, the pleasure is immeasurable and unforgettable.

Mom, Dad, Tracy, Val... Family is fantastic.

Cousin Carol... THANKS FOR EVERYTHING!

for Pam Cruz

TABLE OF CONTENTS

FOREWORD

BRAD LEWIS AND HIS DOUBLE SCULL PARTNER, PAUL ENQUIST, are the only American men to have won an Olympic rowing event in the quarter of a century since the 1964 Olympic Games in Tokyo. *Assault on Lake Casitas* is the amazing story of how Lewis and Enquist reached that summit of athletic performance. Not only is this an entertaining narrative, but Lewis also succeeds in communicating the intensity of focus that fueled and guided his quest for the gold. He provides a rare and illuminating view of one man's path to athletic excellence.

The implicit message of *Assault on Lake Casitas* is that the path to peak performance requires rigorous practice and unbending intent. This approach to athletic training is easy enough to describe in the abstract, but it is extremely difficult to grasp and embrace in practice. Lewis, however, brings abstraction down into the real world and demonstrates the application of this powerful approach to practice through the example of his own experience. He describes with clarity and candor his struggle to maintain a focus of mind and body, moment to moment, in both practice and performance.

The process of athletic training was for Lewis a relentless pursuit of competitive success. Yet, beneath each episode of competition, whether in practice or performance, raged a far more profound and private struggle - a struggle of will. Lewis's intensely personal struggle mirrors the struggles of all who pursue perfection, whatever the discipline. One's competitors are, on this deeper level, merely reflections of one's own possibilities and limitations, of one's strengths and weaknesses, one's hopes and fears. This is the exquisite mystery, and the majesty, that lies at the heart of the sport. It is the mystery of personal exploration. It is the majesty of self-realization through an unending quest for completion.

The challenge of perfection is a potent seduction to the human spirit. Even the first moment of involvement with a discipline such as rowing potentially embodies the promise of perfection. And each incremental advance in strength, or endurance, or technique - each confrontation with and extension of personal limits - hints of some final moment of completion. It is this possibility of perfection, this promise of completion that guides and motivates the practice. The material rewards, the praise and exaltation, although powerful, are secondary.

Intuitively, instinctively, we seem to know that such moments of completion are accessible. For some, the purposeful quest for perfection becomes a passion, even an obsession. It may be that an athlete must be obsessed to achieve the level of performance that Lewis and Enquist attained. Passion is certainly essential. Yet passion and obsession are by no means sufficient. Too often this potent energy is twisted and deflected in the heat of elite competition, as the focus narrows and the intensity builds. Perceptions become distorted. One's opponent becomes a barrier to success rather than an indispensable partner in the pursuit of peak performance. Losses in competition are perceived as defeats at the hands of an adversary rather than failures of one's own will, leading to despair and blame rather than insights and growth. And because personalities and passions frequently are inflated in the heat of competition, their clashes and embraces can be dramatically intensified. The deep mutual respect among competitors - a respect born of shared dreams and fears, of shared exhilaration, fatigue and frustration - may be forgotten, lost in the fervor of the competitive moment. Put simply, navigation in the rarefied atmosphere of consummate practice and elite competition is profoundly difficult. Everywhere there are distractions and seductions that threaten to blunt or deflect the focus.

Passion simply is not enough. It must be harnessed to the will. Then, through a relentless exercise of will, this energy must be brought to a focus of maximum intensity, and the point of focus must be directed with precision and purpose within each successive present moment of practice. If left unharnessed, the passion to excel will deflect the mind from its focus on the present moment of practice, moment to moment, day to day. Properly focused, passion can propel the practitioner to the edge of perfection.

Assault on Lake Casitas charts Lewis's course in his pursuit of perfection. It is by no means a straight and narrow path. It is a path paved with defeats. Along the way, there were mistakes of judgment and failures of will. There were dead ends and detours, distractions and seductions. But Lewis persevered, even when seemingly lost in the depths of adversity. He rose from each failure stronger and more focused in mind and body. And ultimately, in concert with his doubles partner, he reached the summit of his discipline.

Lewis analogizes his quest for completion to the assembling of a great puzzle. On August 5, 1984, in the finals of the Olympic doubles competition, the puzzle came together for Lewis and Enquist in a performance that flirted with perfection.

In these precious moments of peak performance, Lewis and Enquist's years of practice found expression as a unified whole that was vastly greater than the sum of its parts. And then these magical, almost religious moments of near perfect wholeness were gone.

The center could not hold. The monumental force of will that bound the puzzle pieces in perfect sync for those few minutes of peak performance could exist only in the present moment of total focus. And as the puzzle fell apart into its pieces, and as the pieces themselves gradually disintegrated over the months and years following those glorious moments of completion, this simple truth emerged: the force of will that binds the puzzle is found only in the focus of mind within the present moment. It is this truth that lurks between the lines of *Assault on Lake Casitas*. It is a truth that cannot be learned too often or too well.

Michael Livingston, Esq.
1972 Olympic silver medalist
April 1990

ASSAULT ON LAKE CASITAS

1

THE ASSAULT BEGINS
5:13 A.M., SUNDAY, JANUARY 15, 1984

ICE COLD JANUARY MORNING. DAN STRUGGLED OVER THE
rattling gate, making the chain and lock bang against the pole,
but no one interrupted our illegal assault. No one passed our
way or heard our self-denigrating laughter as we realized we
looked more like bums, with our tattered shirts and leggings,
than two aspiring Olympians.

I carefully handed my single scull over the gate to Dan. He
took it from me and then set it on a grassy slope a few yards
away. We repeated the maneuver with his boat, and then I
passed him our oars. I took my time as I climbed over, being
extra careful not to lose my balance as my groin traversed the
sharp wire teeth along the top of the gate.

At 5:30 A.M., temperature about 38 degrees, a stiff wind
blowing from the south, we gathered our equipment and
hurried toward the lake. Our 'Assault on Lake Casitas,' as we
had decided to call it, had begun.

Our purpose in coming to this distant place at so peculiar
an hour was to tap into the source of all rowing energy for

1984 - Lake Casitas, the site of the rowing events for the Los Angeles Olympic Games. We were also in search of a Brad Lewis-style adventure, something wild, unprecedented, a break from the predictable and often boring rigors of training.

Once inside the forbidden sanctuary, my senses turned on edge, exactly the way I liked to feel. I glanced frequently at the road, but I knew a quick escape would be impossible with our delicate boats. We had to move carefully, keep low to the ground, and, if discovered, be prepared to split up, like they do in my favorite reruns of *Rat Patrol*.

I wondered what would happen if we were caught by the rangers who relentlessly patrolled the lake in search of trespassers. Lake Casitas served as a drinking water reservoir for Ventura County, and therefore, swimming, skiing, jet-skiing, wading, washing, splashing, frolicking, and sculling was illegal. The prospect of our skinny boats tipping over and our unclean bodies polluting the sacred waters made the rangers furious. The Lake Casitas guardians had decreed that only two exceptions would be made to their 'No Sculling' law: the Pre-Olympic Regatta and the Olympic Games themselves.

A few months earlier, in September, I had raced at the Pre-Olympic Regatta. Since Lake Casitas had never hosted a regatta of any size, much less the Olympics, a practice competition was needed to ensure that the buoys would be in place and that the water would not be too rough for afternoon rowing. For this mock-Olympics, only the single and double scull events were contested, along with the straight pair and four-with coxswain.

A more accurate name for the competition might have been the Pre-Olympic Party, since the regatta took place only two weeks after the '83 World Championships, the premiere event in rowing outside of the Olympics. Many of the competitors who arrived in California for the Pre-Olympics were tired of training. They were more interested in seeing Disneyland and learning to surf.

I too was tired, but I had a special reason for eagerly anticipating this regatta. My partner, Paul Enquist, and I had raced the double scull at the '83 World Championships - and had finished dead last in the finals. Now, at the Pre-Olympics, we were presented with that rarest of opportunities in the sporting world, a second chance. We'd use it to prove that we were capable of racing, stroke for stroke, against the faster double scullers in the world.

Before the finals of the Pre-Olympics, Paul and I had decided on a new strategy. We'd row like maniacs for the first half - 1000 meters. Then, with a handsome lead and all our opponents wondering what the hell we had eaten for breakfast, we would sell our souls to stay ahead until the finish line - 2000 meters, a mile and a quarter. The distance was not far if you were flying overhead in a jet plane. It was roughly the distance to the moon if you were getting hammered, your ass handed to you, waked down and left behind, severely bruised and beaten.

The first part of our strategy worked to perfection. At the halfway mark, we led every top double scull team in the world by a full boat length of open water. Then the bed broke. First the Norwegians passed us, then the East Germans, followed by the Finnish double. Paul and I would have needed an extra set of lungs and legs to stay ahead. By the time we limped across the finish line, every boat except the Italians, two lightweight scullers, had passed us. A minute or two later, after being ordered by the race officials to vacate the finish line area - only medalists need stay around - we slowly paddled back to the dock, barely able to hang onto our oars.

As I listened to the medals being awarded to the Norwegians, I swore that I would never row the double scull again - not with Paul Enquist, not with anyone. My rowing future would be decided in the single scull, the one-man boat. You make your own success in the single scull. You win or lose by your own toughness. You alone are responsible for the outcome of the race. The sheer, unadulterated pleasure of winning a single sculling race, regardless of the level, from novice to elite, is enough to keep you training for another three years.

On this Sunday morning, the Pre-Olympic regatta was ancient history. A fresh year, a new year, the Olympic year, had finally arrived. Never before had I welcomed with such anticipation a specific sequence of numbers: one, nine, eight, four. 1984.

I tightened my oarlocks, put my right foot between the tracks, and with my left foot, I lightly pushed away from the shore. I have always loved the brief, exquisite moment when I freed myself from the constraints of land. Such a simple thing - push and glide - yet so wonderfully liberating.

I shivered, and my feet burned with a million pinpricks from having stood in the icy water. As I pulled on my socks I looked around me, trying to separate the limitless night sky from the lake surface. The water was so dark it appeared to have no depth, no bottom, as though I were sitting on a black cloud. I paddled toward the middle of the lake, gliding on the forbidden pool, hidden, unseen, in a cocoon. I closed my eyes for a few strokes and let the curtain drop completely.

I had begun rowing in high school, continued through college, and then another seven years - a grand total of 13 years. Through all those watery miles, and all those weights lifted, and all those hills run, I had been spiraling toward this tiny pond. Rowing, for me, had become a painful, most persistent itch that had gradually taken over my life. I would win the gold medal or die trying. The phrase 'die trying' might sound corny, but when you expend an immeasurable amount of effort over 13 years, all toward a solitary goal, then a commitment to die trying is a natural evolution. Were it any other way, the time you spent rowing would have been wasted.

As the stars began to release their grip on the sky, I turned around and looked for Dan's dark outline. Our row would be short this morning, roughly the same time and distance as the Olympic single scull finals, 2000 meters. Before leaving the shore, Dan and I had agreed to hold a pretend Olympic final, complete with starting commands in French, the international language of rowing.

A few minutes later, as we sat poised at the starting line, I gave the commands: "East Germany, prêt?" I couldn't imagine an Olympic final without an East German. They were always fast, and they won an inordinate number of medals.

"Finland, prêt?" The great Finnish sculler, Pertti Karppinen, '76 and '80 Olympic champion, would certainly be favored to win.

"West Germany, prêt?" At the '76 Montreal Olympics, from the standing room only side of the racecourse, I had watched the West German sculler, Peter-Michael Kolbe, lead the whole race, only to be passed by Karppinen in the last five strokes. This race made a serious impression on me. I was in awe of these titans, and I immediately wanted to join the battle. Within a few days, I had acquired a racing shell of my own, and before a year had passed, this obscure, antiquated sport had become my passion.

"Dan Louis, prêt?" He nodded and said nothing. Dan was my training partner and good friend. We both claimed to be six feet, four inches tall, although in honesty I needed a pair of cowboy boots to break the 76-inch barrier. In rowing, taller is better. We each weighed over 190 pounds, for which no pretending was required. Usually, both Dan and I needed a shave.

"Brad Lewis, prêt?" Believe it.

"Etes vous prêt? Partez!" On the word 'Partez,' we charged through the rough water, spray flying, oars slapping, each of us trying to forge a lead in the early going. Dan hung tough. Although younger than me by five years, Dan was already an Olympic caliber sculler, and he always tried his hardest. I also tried hard, and I hated to lose. At the 1000-meter mark, I had a one-length lead.

In my imagination, Karppinen was ahead of me by half a length, but I was catching him. Was he sick? Too old, perhaps? Not me. I was hungry, angry - the best combination. With 20 strokes, to go I pulled even. Drive the legs, squeeze off the finish, more pressure, push the rating up another beat. Two more strokes, and on my last surge I drove past Karppinen and crossed the finish line in first place.

I slumped over my oars, fighting to catch my breath in the cold air. As I waited for Dan to come alongside, my homemade steam began to rise from every pore. We had rowed a good hard race.

The 1984 Olympic single scull trials would take place on May 5 - four long months away. I wished they were tomorrow. After the single trials, another three months loomed until the Opening Ceremonies. Three thousand miles of continuous practice stretched in front of me like an endless ocean. Through all those miles, I had to nurture the sweet sensations I had felt this morning - unrelenting pursuit, complete abandon, consuming anger, grinding out the strokes, right through the finish.

2

Wᴇᴛ Bᴇɢɪɴɴɪɴɢs

Sᴄᴜʟʟɪɴɢ ɪs ᴀ ʀᴇᴍᴀʀᴋᴀʙʟʏ sɪᴍᴘʟᴇ ᴅɪsᴄɪᴘʟɪɴᴇ.

To learn the basics of the sport, head down to Sears and buy a 12-foot aluminum rowboat and a pair of oars. Toss the boat into the nearest lake or river, set the oars in the locks, and blast off.

Immediately you'll notice a problem - you're facing backward. Like the tug-of-war, an Olympic sport in the early 1900s, and the backstroke in swimming, a sculler needs an intuitive sense of direction. Some scullers twist their heads around every stroke to check for watery obstructions, while others simply point their boat down the course and hope for the best. In theory all scullers must keep the land on their starboard side so boats going in opposite directions will pass each other like cars on a freeway. Unfortunately, no center divider exists on a winding river. Every practitioner of the sculling game eventually collides with something - a bridge abutment, a navigational buoy - pray it's not another sculler.

After a few minutes, your arms and lower back will begin to tire and a small blister will form on the palm of your hand.

Welcome to the world of sculling. But unlike your Sears row-boat, a competitive scull has wheels mounted underneath the seat. The seat rolls on a pair of grooved, 30-inch tracks. The addition of the rolling seat allows you to power each stroke with your legs, the strongest muscles in your body.

The stroke is divided into two complementary segments, the drive and the recovery. The drive propels the boat through the water. The recovery allows an oarsman to move from the end of the stroke, the release, to the beginning of the stroke, the catch. The drive is all muscle, strength, eye-popping effort. The recovery is cool, subtle, a chance to take a deep breath and prepare for the next drive.

The driving effort is carefully quantified in the psyche of every practicing oarsman: half-power is like walking up a flight of stairs; three-quarter power is the same as a steady jog up those stairs; full-power is the equivalent of running to the top of Mt. Whitney. Then comes race-power. This is a special category, reserved for the ultimate in physical expression. At the completion of the final stroke of a close race, an oarsman should collapse over his oars, having spent every possible ounce of energy. Fainting from exhaustion at the finish line, although rarely seen, is greatly respected among competitors.

On a warm, Newport Beach, Saturday afternoon, October 1970, I drove to the Orange Coast College boathouse with my brother, Tracy, who is three years older. He had an appointment to meet with Steve Reichert, the team's best rower. Tracy was a strong oarsman, but his rough technique had kept him out of the first boat. Tracy hoped that an hour's practice on the rowing machines, under Steve's watchful eye, could whip his technique into shape. Steve and Tracy were close friends, and now decades later they are still close friends. Rowing relationships, it seems, last a lifetime. I've met most of my own best friends, Zimmer, Clark, Fletcher, Roop, Tricia Smith, at the boathouse.

While Tracy and Steve practiced on the rowing machines, I walked around the deserted boathouse, looking at the beautifully crafted eight-man shells. The smooth, deep varnish was like a mirror on the skin of the wooden boats, and as I rubbed my hand over the surface, I could see my own distorted reflection trapped in the sheen. I walked to the end of the boathouse to inspect the oars, standing at attention like patient soldiers. The wooden handles had been worn smooth over the months and years.

Above my head a half-dozen single sculls hung from the rafters.

"How would you like to try sculling?" Steve asked when they had finished their workout. "You can use one of the training singles. I'll help you put it on the water."

Steve carefully lowered a red and white trainer from the rafters. The scull descended from the heavens, and my life was never the same. The boat, a relatively clumsy, 50-pound beast, seemed to me an unbelievably sleek craft, ideal for exploring the harbor's nooks and crannies. I'd found my escape vehicle of choice, the perfect solution for a young man, not yet old enough to drive, but already searching for his freedom.

"Remember," he said, as I gingerly climbed into the boat, "the left hand goes over the right, and keep your thumbs over the ends of the oar handles. It's simple. Left over right, and thumbs over the ends. Use the oars like trainer wheels - let them scrape across the water and you won't tip over. Don't worry, I'll hold onto the stern, until you get a feel for the balance."

With my bow pointed into the harbor, I practiced a few tentative strokes. My balance felt most precarious at the catch, when my oars were almost parallel to the boat. When I glanced up after a few strokes, I suddenly realized that Steve was now 30 feet away. He had let go of the stern. My first sculling lesson was now complete: left hand over right, thumbs over the ends of the oar handles, and most important, keep my head up.

I could hear Steve and Tracy laughing as I scuttled across the channel using tight little stokes. I managed to stay upright, which surprised them both, since many scullers tip over on their first outing. As I began to feel as though I'd mastered the balance, the driver of a 45-foot motorboat opened up the throttle. Three huge waves marched across the channel, straight toward me. I managed to keep my boat upright through the first wave, but the second wave struck before I had recovered. In a blink I tipped over. I swam my boat to the dock, emptied it out, and went back for more. I was 15 years old at the time of my sculling baptism.

Sculling is for individualists. I have it in my lineage, my genes, my soul, this rare characteristic. The whole Lewis family, brother Tracy, sister Val, mom Bernice, and dad David, are all individualists, all champions, ultra dependable, loyal beyond belief. I have been blessed with an amazing, wonderful family. Dad, a Los Angeles native, 27 years with Transamerica Insurance as a sales rep, won a silver medal at the Pan American Games for Seniors track and field in the 800 meters. He rowed at UCLA for a short time after returning from the Second World War, or more specifically, after returning from duty aboard the *Fanshaw Bay*, where he fought in the Battle of Leyte Gulf. Mom, from Redwood City, worked in Yosemite as a ranger. In fact, that's where my mother and father met after the war. She was a lover of long walks along the beach in the early morning. Tracy is the hardest worker of us kids, always pulling his own weight and more. Val is perhaps the toughest, a California Highway Patrolwoman for a few years, working the South L.A. district at night, a challenge exceeding anything found in the world of sports. Tracy, Val, Mom, and Dad understood, enjoyed, and wholly supported my peculiar passion for sculling.

During the latter half of my junior year at Corona del Mar High School, I joined the rowing team. We had a wild team, made up of burned-out, bored, and generally cast-off athletes from water polo, football, track, baseball, cross-country, and tennis. One of these athletes was a young shot-putter-turned-rower named Curtis Fleming, with whom I shared the sport for over a decade. Our team worked hard, we had an incredible amount of fun, and we even won a few races against second freshman college teams.

On my high school team I learned about the other side of the sport - sweep rowing. As commonly practiced by college crew teams, and most often seen on beer commercials, the sweep rower uses only one oar, as in sweeping the floor with a broom. Unlike sculling, sweep rowing is a team sport, requiring at least two rowers to make the boat go straight. The boat of choice by many sweep oarsmen is the eight-oared shell, often referred to as rowings 'glamour boat.' My idea of glamour is the single scull, although in truth the concept of glamour should not be used in conjunction with any type of rowing. On every level, and in every size boat, rowing is a modest sport.

Both types of rowing, sweep and sculling, suited me well. I was outdoors; I could work as hard as I wanted; and no substitutions were allowed. Our coach, Mark Sandusky, couldn't call time-out and take me out of the action in the middle of a race, as so often happened when I played on the basketball team my freshman and sophomore years. Best of all, the rhythm of a properly rowed stroke felt incredibly satisfying - a sexual rhythm. It felt good.

Our high school team practiced at the University of California, Irvine boathouse. On many afternoons I borrowed a single scull from the college and paddled around the bay. The boat, an old Pocock fiberglass trainer, had a hundred miniature leaks along the hull, and by the time I returned to the dock, I was practically rowing underwater. Those were the good ol' days. I wasn't preparing for the Olympics. I sculled because I loved it.

I eventually attended U.C. Irvine, gaining entrance through an athletic deferment, which was made possible because of my high school rowing. While at Irvine, I continued to sweep row, but with marginal success. The team had one good season - 1974. Coach Bob Ernst and varsity stroke Bruce Ibbetson, both future Olympians, led the team to a dozen victories. Unfortunately, I was not on the varsity during these halcyon days, toiling instead on the lowly junior varsity. Soon after the '74 season, Bob Ernst left U.C. Irvine to coach at a better rowing school, the University of Washington, and the Irvine program quickly sank into mediocrity.

At Irvine I again rowed a single scull whenever I had a free afternoon. By this time I'd moved up in equipment, thanks to Duvall Hecht, who lent me the use of his beautiful wooden Pocock. Duvall, the originator of UCI's crew, was a gold medalist at the '56 Melbourne Olympics in the pair-without coxswain, a boat comprised of two sweep rowers and no coxswain or steersman.

I loved the simplicity of sculling. No one was to blame for a bad stroke. No one got mad at me when I was late for practice. If things didn't go well, I had no one to look to but myself.

I quit the crew my senior year at Irvine, 1976, and for nearly one full year, I stayed away from the sport. Then I went to the Montreal Olympic Games and saw for myself what real rowing was all about. Soon after the Games, I came back to the sport of rowing, single sculling to be specific, and trained with a vengeance.

The next year, 1977, I drove to Philadelphia for the sole purpose of racing against the fastest scullers in the country. I was perhaps the most eager, ambitious, energetic West Coaster ever to descend on the staid rowing fraternity of Boathouse Row. My timing could not have been better. Since it was a post-Olympic year, many of the top scullers had recently retired. The door was open for new scullers like me to win a few races. I also found out how small the sculling fraternity was in the United States. At the national championships, only eleven scullers were entered in the elite competition. I finished fourth.

Toward the end of that summer, I earned a place on the national rowing team as stroke of the U.S. quadruple scull, four scullers in one boat. When we arrived at the '77 World Rowing Championships in Amsterdam, I felt as though I were in Disneyland for the first time. My heroes, the legends of rowing, the Hansen brothers, Dreifke, Kolbe, were all around me. I saw the East German team march into the boat launching area, singing their national anthem. They looked like angry robots displaying Iron German Discipline at its finest. I was impressed.

Eventually our quadruple scull finished ninth at the Worlds. Ninth was better than tenth, but still a long way from the finals, much less a gold medal. But overall the whole '77 season gave me a strong sense of confidence and inspiration.

In April of the next year, 1978, on the drive back to Seattle (where I was training at the time) from the San Diego Crew Classic, I broke my right leg and partially severed the patella tendon in a foolish accident.

In an instant, I went from preparing for the '78 single scull trials to enduring two long months in a full leg cast, followed by a long, painful convalescence. Once out of the cast, the adhesions that had formed around the knee joint had to be severed. I've never encountered anything to compare with that excruciating pain. I finished 1978 wholly out of shape, weak, and generally unhappy. I had to begin my rowing career all over again.

I had a wild notion the following spring that I'd be happier in Europe. One day in June 1979, I packed up my oars, scraped together a few hundred dollars, and flew to West Germany. I wish I had taken more pictures during my trip, to capture the people I met and the fun I had. I didn't win many races, but I held my own.

In 1980 I rowed in the Olympic quadruple scull, but we never had a chance to determine our ultimate speed. President Jimmy Carter, who probably never rowed a day in his life, made his unforgivable decision to boycott the '80 Moscow Olympic Games. Regardless of the boycott, I kept rowing. I was only 25 years old at the time, and my best races were still ahead of me.

Three years later I raced the double scull with Paul Enquist at the '83 World Championships. We made the finals, which was excellent, but then we placed a distant sixth.

In seven years I had made three national teams. I had never won a national championship in any boat. I had not won many races outside of California. Along the way I had acquired three single sculls, five sets of oars, a '72 V8 Mercury

Montego, and some impressive calluses on my hands. Although I did not lack for determination or equipment, my climb up the ladder of sculling success had been slow and tedious. This year, 1984, promised to be better.

To earn a place on the '84 U.S. Olympic sculling team, an oarsman had to win the Olympic trials in either the single, double, or quadruple scull. The single trials were to be held in early May, with the double and quad trials in July. After the single trials, an official sculling camp was to be convened. The double and quad selected at this camp would then attempt to defeat all challengers at their respective trials. In recent years the camp boats usually dominated the Olympic or World Championship trials, thanks to their superior coaching, excellent equipment, and ample funding, not to mention having the best athletes. But upsets had been known to occur.

The Olympic single scull trials, by contrast, were wide open.

Brad Alan Lewis

3

ARRIVING, THE OLYMPIC SINGLE TRIALS
APRIL 29, 1984

FOLLOWING OUR DETAILED BLUEPRINT FOR VICTORY,
my trainer, Mitch Lewis, and I left southern California exactly
five days before the first preliminary race of the Olympic single
scull trials that would be held in Princeton, New Jersey. For
an event of this importance, I wanted a few extra days to
adjust to the time change.

In Newark, New Jersey, we rented a car and drove straight
to the Princeton Ramada Inn, on the outskirts of town. I had
purposely chosen this hotel because I was certain my
opponents would be staying a few miles away at the less
expensive Scanticon Hotel. I wanted to be away from the
traditional locker room camaraderie that was such a large part
of the rowing world. This camaraderie had bypassed my part
of town, or maybe I had bypassed it. Either way, I knew I'd be
happier if we stayed at the Ramada.

By choice I trained in the distant rowing outpost of
Newport Beach, while my opponents huddled in tight cliques,
mostly in Boston and Philadelphia. I belonged to no cliques

or clubs other than my own, the Newport Beach Rowing Club, of which I was the sole member. To some extent the wall between myself and my opponents was an artificial device that I had constructed in the past year. At the previous summer's World Championships, for example, I had been relatively well accepted by my teammates. We drank beers together, gossiped about other rowers, and talked about women. Team camaraderie, at least from my experience, consisted of little else.

This year was different. First, I intended to race the single scull rather than the double or quad. Single sculling was a one-man show. The single sculler had to be ornery, independent, and stingy with his energy and patience. Second, I was contending for a place on the Olympic team, as opposed to the World Championship team. The Worlds are prestigious, difficult, and attended by every top rowing country. The Olympics are magic.

Time is marked by the passing of the Games: Mexico City, Munich, Montreal, Moscow. Because of age or some other circumstance, an athlete might have only one Olympiad in which to prove himself. I needed to maintain the highest level of passion in order to reach my solitary goal: representing the U.S. in the single scull at the 1984 Los Angeles Olympic Games.

My self-imposed exile had certain disadvantages. I had no close friends or allies among the other scullers to help break the tension. But it did have one great advantage. Since I trained alone, the other scullers had no idea of my true speed, which I felt had greatly improved over last year.

My new speed came from killer strength. I'd spent a thousand hours in Gilham's Gym over the past two years, shaping my body into a new form-pure powerlifter, thick-chested, thick-necked, legs like Eric Heiden. Steroids, gimmicks, and shortcuts were not part of my regimen. Instead, I paid for each new ounce of muscle the old-fashioned way - intense weight lifting sessions, three times a week, multiplied by months and now years.

In a few days, I would claim my reward, leading the best scullers in the country, watching them flounder in my small but annoying wake as I sped toward the finish line and victory. Rowing is such a fine sport. Everyone goes backward, and the leader can see his opponents as they struggle in vain.

I especially wanted to avoid one person who I expected would also be staying at the Scanticon Hotel - the Olympic sculling coach, Harry Parker. I had known Harry Parker a long time, ten years this summer, and like most oarsmen, I had acquired only a few rare insights into the man. My sense of Harry Parker came solely from personal observation and from the countless secondhand stories that I'd heard. To me, he seemed like a wizard capable of piercing even the strongest armor. He had done it all - single sculler at the Rome Olympics in 1960, coach of a dozen champion crews during his reign at Harvard, and coach of Olympic and international medalist crews. He was and is and will always be a legend in the sport of rowing. The only prize he had never won, either as a coach or competitor, was an Olympic gold medal.

Harry didn't know what to make of me. I was too West Coast, too skittish, too flaky, simply too weird for his taste. He liked solid, proven, reliable competitors. He was the master of the one or two word comment designed to send your mind off on a tangent, wondering what the hell he meant. Then halfway down the racecourse, you'd suddenly think, 'He meant I didn't have a chance.' Harry was the great destroyer of concentration unless, of course, he was your coach, and then you would walk through flaming fire to reach your goal, confident that victory was your birthright. Some good books are waiting to be written about Coach Harry Parker.

My main opponent at the Olympic trials, Tiff Wood, had been coached at Harvard by Harry Parker. Although Harry was not Tiff's coach this year, he was definitely on Tiff's side, and definitely not on my side. Other competitors were also tied to Harry Parker - Charlie Altekruse, Bill Purdy, Joe Bouscaren, John Biglow. 'Harry's Boys' I called them. I was not one of them. To keep my life simple, I chose to stay away from the grizzled warrior and his boys.

After unpacking, Mitch and I drove to the Princeton University boathouse in search of the truck that had brought my single scull from home. I wanted a quick row before dinner to loosen the kinks from the long flight. The vintage Dodge pick-up truck, its roof rack jammed with boats, was parked under a huge maple tree. During the '78 World Championship single trials, I had pitched a small tent under this tree when I lacked enough money to afford even the cheapest motel. In '78, I didn't make the semi-finals. Times had changed. I now had money to pay for hotels - and I was going to win.

On top of the truck, hidden under its canvas cover and wrapped like a mummy with ten pounds of duct tape, was my single scull, 27 feet long, 30 pounds fully rigged, a blend of fiberglass, Kevlar, and carbon fiber, with a little stainless steel mixed in to hold it all together. A week before, I had strapped my single onto the roof of this pick-up truck next to a half-dozen boats belonging to other West Coast scullers. A young rower, for whom money was more dear than time, spent four days driving from Newport Beach to Princeton. A few years ago I would have made the drive, but now I was older, less patient, and maybe a tad wiser. I now insisted on flying, regardless of the cost. A dozen cross-country trips had taught me a simple lesson. The effects of sitting in the cab of a noisy pick-up truck, for a hundred nonstop hours, was a good way to ensure that your hard-earned strength and endurance would be divided in half.

After some quick rigging, I was ready to lay claim to the racecourse. The Lake Carnegie rowing course was like a rough edged swimming pool, inflated to absurd dimensions: two thousand meters long, a hundred yards across, with six lines of buoys evenly dividing the course. Thick trees and bushes, energized by the wild spring profusion, covered every inch of shoreline. If you sat still for a few minutes, you could almost see the leaves growing. Lazy turtles rested on half-submerged logs. Gnats and flies and other buzzing creatures provided constant background music. Lake Carnegie was amazingly beautiful, especially when you consider that Trenton, Newark, and other less picturesque locales were only a few minutes away.

I needed a half-dozen laps to relearn the landmarks: the giant sloping rock at 750 meters, the small white sign at 1000 meters, the lakefront mansion at 1500 meters, and the all important 'white shed' at 1850 meters - roughly thirty seconds to go in the race. By memorizing the landmarks, I could glance at the shore at any point and know my position, at least in theory. My vision had a tendency to blur in the latter stages of a tough race.

Equally important, I needed the laps to relearn the art of rowing on a buoyed course. My practice course in Newport Beach was not blessed with buoys, and over the months I had acquired a tendency to wander outside the boundaries of my imagined lane. Many scullers, myself included, had met their match, not against other rowers, but in fighting these protruding Styrofoam annoyances. In my first sculling races, I struggled against the buoys, careening from side to side like a bumper car gone haywire. The sequence is familiar to all novices: the buoy is clipped, the oar handle suddenly ejects from your grasp, you experience a frantic burst of terror as you realize you're probably going to tip over, perspiration stings your eyes, and lastly, you try to reclaim your oar while everyone in the race zooms past.

But during this evening's exploration of the course, without the distraction or fatigue of a race, my single scull ran straight and true down the heart of the lane.

Thirty-five scullers had entered the Olympic trials. Six heats would be held, with the winner of each heat going directly to the semifinals. The top three finishers in each of the two semi-finals would advance to the finals. The winner of the finals would be designated as the U.S. Olympic single sculler.

The regatta started on Friday. Five endless days dragged past. I had plenty of time to get nervous and to contemplate my most recent major race, the Pre-Olympic Regatta, held nine months ago. Paul Enquist and I had raced the double scull - raced poorly. Now, I kept telling myself, I was in my rightful place, the single scull.

Suddenly, just when I thought they would never arrive, the Olympic single trials began.

Heat number 5 was to start in exactly three minutes. By official decree, one 'seeded' sculler was placed in each of the six heats. The other lanes were filled by scullers chosen at random. Based on some intangible criterion, the regatta officials had selected me to be one of the seeded scullers. I was happy to be included in this group, since I could now assume that my opposition in this preliminary race would not be especially tough.

As I looked across the lanes, I reviewed my strategy: get ahead and stay ahead. I wanted to build a huge lead in the first minute in order to discourage the other scullers. Once my opponents realized the race was lost, they would conserve their remaining energy for tomorrow's repêchage, or second chance race.

A danger existed in this strategy. If one of my opponents, unaware of his need to conserve energy, or worse, an unknown but legitimately fast sculler, did not ease off in the latter stages, and if I were extra tired from having spent too much energy in the early going, this novice could row through me. I had been a fast novice during my first year of sculling, so I knew these characters did exist.

The dreary grey sky provided the perfect cover for my ultimate attack on the sculling world. I was hyper-excited in the last few moments before the start. The referee's launch had stopped growling. I looked over my shoulder, down the racecourse. From this perspective, the finish line seemed to melt into the horizon. A duck splashed about, ignoring the solemnity of the moment. Voices from the nearby shore floated crystal clear across the water. I pretended to ignore the outside world, but actually I absorbed every ounce of information with the speed of a computer. I have always loved the last few seconds before the start of a race.

"Partez." I flew off the starting line, high and hard, a little too high and definitely too hard, but I was ahead. At the 500-meter mark, I had a one-length lead over Charlie Altekruse, a good sculler from Harvard, with the other scullers trailing far behind. Charlie kept up the chase for another 700 meters, and then he too eased off and paddled the rest of the course. As soon as I noticed that the puddles at the ends of Charlie's oars had shrunk in size, I shifted into half-power, and cruised to the finish line.

In the evening, my trainer, Mitch Lewis, earned his keep by giving me some hard massage and lots of encouraging talk. This was our first voyage together, although I had known Mitch my whole life. In addition to being my trainer, Mitch was also my first cousin on my father's side.

Mitch was 37 years old and getting pudgy around the middle, but I knew from Gilham's Gym that he could out-lift me in every weight room test of strength. Some of my earliest memories were of Christmas dinner at his father's house in Altadena. I used to wander with my brother into Mitch's room, to look at the precisely detailed model airplanes that hung from the ceiling, twisting slowly in the shadows of the December twilight. When I was older, I tried to assemble my own models, but invariably I glued on the wheels before I had the fuselage together. I seemed to lack the patience for detail work.

After college, Mitch discovered rugby and martial arts. Both disciplines gave Mitch a place to express his true nature. Mitch studied Karate, Judo, Aikido, and several other disciplines, and now he could do serious damage to anyone with his own scary array of techniques and implements.

Mitch's greatest pride was his skill as a trainer, and without a doubt, Mitch knew his trade. In the sport of Judo, his specialty was mid-match repairs. Like a one-man pit crew, he would rush onto the mat to aid a fallen player, pulling from his satchel all manner of tapes, splints, and pain-deadening balms. Unfortunately for Mitch - twice a family man, home, Harley Davidson, and Great Dane owner - his work with Judo players and rowers paid him nothing.

Besides playing the role of my confidant, Mitch supplied two other fantastic skills: massage therapy, and, even better, aura balancing. The benefits of massage are well known -

increased blood flow and speedy venting of excess lactic acid. Every East German athlete, from obscure junior to Olympian, has access to a masseur.

Aura balancing is an exotic, semi-magical, Eastern-derived discipline. It draws together your scattered energy and out-of-control thoughts, and somehow focuses both entities like a laser beam. Mitch could make this hour, this very moment, the best of your athletic life.

The next afternoon I survived the semi-finals, although only by inches, due to a blazing fast start and a remarkably slow finish. With only inches to spare, I finished third in my semi-final, once again defeating Charlie Altekruse. I had advanced to the finals, which was all I cared about.

In the other semi-final, my two main opponents, Tiff Wood and John Biglow, qualified for the finals with much less trouble. They sculled comfortably across the finish line with lengths to spare, like the champions they could rightly claim to be.

Tiff was a tightly wound brute, shorter than most world-class scullers, lean and very strong, full of energy and naughti-ness. He had graduated from St. Paul's Prep School and Harvard University without having developed the slightest reservations about burping, farting, or sucking his thumb. At the '83 Worlds, Tiff had won the bronze medal in the single scull. He was favored by the press, most onlookers, and by himself, to win tomorrow's final.

John Biglow, known as 'Biggy' to everyone, of Seattle and Yale, was an equally tough opponent. To many people he seemed like a peculiar young man. A faraway look in his eyes gave some observers the impression, usually unrewarded, that he was about to say something extremely important. I knew from having spent a few summers with Biggy that his odd behavior was mostly an act, a parlor game he played to keep from getting bored.

Somewhere in Biggy's eccentric lineage, he had acquired a glorious insensitivity to pain that allowed him to row harder than anyone in the world. Despite an awkward style and a complete lack of international sculling experience, Biggy had won the bronze medal in the single scull at the '81 World Championships. In 1982 he dumbfounded the experts by repeating the same accomplishment. He was totally fearless.

I had never represented the U.S. in single sculls at the World Championships or at the Olympics. I had dreamed of it a million times, but nothing more.

4

DEATH AT THE SINGLE TRIALS
8:30 A.M., SUNDAY, MAY 6, 1984

As I PUSHED OFF FROM THE DOCK, MITCH SAID, "TODAY IS a good day to die." I nodded, and paddled a few strokes. Yes, a good day to die. I liked the phrasing. Not often can a man pinpoint the day, the place, the exact time of his death. Possessing this knowledge calmed my spinning head. I was going to die to win this race - no doubt about it - so I need not think beyond the moment. Let it happen, exactly as I had written in my notebook and rehearsed a thousand times. I was willing, body, mind, and soul, to pay the price.

Then Mitch screamed "OO-SO," our private little psyche yell, which loosely translated into 'Kick some ass.' I yelled "OO-SO" back to him, loud and strong, and full of home-grown sincerity. Then I paddled toward the starting line for the finals of the Olympic single scull trials.

Mitch had borrowed *OO-SO* from Judo. It was intended to heighten my concentration, and as a side effect, I'm sure our screaming convinced all listeners that Mitch and I were a couple of strange characters. I had no qualms about being labeled as strange, unconventional, even bizarre, just so long as my critics also included such words as intense, devoted, and wholly passionate about achieving my goal.

All week long I had spoken as little as possible to my opponents. What could they do for me? My goal was selfish, and I refused to pretend it was otherwise. Of course, my opponents sought the identical goal, but somehow they found a way to be social and friendly in the process. Perhaps my training-in-exile had deprived me of this ability. Or perhaps my selfishness was the reason I trained in exile. Despite the reason, solitude and selfishness had become so intertwined over the last year that they could not be separated. I would have plenty of time after the race, I told myself, for backslapping, handshaking, and casual banter.

They, the incestuous they, the other scullers competing at the trials, along with their friends, girlfriends, and other spectators, had watched me with great amusement as I made my way from the car to the dock, always shadowed by Madman Mitch. They talked among themselves about my latest tricks, which included taking my boat to the Ramada Inn each night, as an extra security measure. As I rowed to the starting line, I felt intense pleasure at the thought of executing my final trick - an impressive victory in the single trials - in front of the ever-present 'they.'

"To the stake boats, please," the starter said. Reluctant for some, hungry and anxious for others, we tucked ourselves into the stake boats, and waited for the fun to begin. I listened as the starter polled the scullers: "Lane one, prêt? Lane two, prêt?" I had the outside lane, leaving me most vulnerable to the crisp headwind that blew directly up the racecourse. Let the wind blow. My new strength was developed especially for headwinds.

"Lane six, prêt?" I was ready a thousand times over.

"Etes vous prêt? Partez!" I drove off the starting line, and after two strokes, I climbed inside myself. I was going to take it easy for a few minutes, while the others tussled among themselves. I felt cool in the early going, supercool to be exact, and I didn't worry when Joe Bouscaren, in the next lane, opened up a two-length lead.

I looked across the course at the 500-meter mark. Good. Excellent. I was right in the middle of the pack, yet barely hurting. A motorboat carrying an ABC film crew was a few yards off my stern, their camera pointed in my direction. In my optimistic, aggressive state of mind, I mouthed the words, "Get your fucking launch away from me." I had worked for years to be in this place, and I didn't want any unnecessary distractions.

At the halfway mark I took three deep breaths, sucking heavy on the air. Then I began to lean on it. I leaned hard, and then I leaned some more. I used my back like a giant lever to pry my boat across the water. I caught the leader, Joe Bouscaren, in 20 strokes, and now I was in first place. With each press of my legs, I pulled farther ahead. Yes, I felt pain. By the 1500-meter mark, my body was wrapped in barbed wire. But if I was hurting, my opponents must have been hurting even more. I welcomed the pain.

In the last 500, I began to count 'tens,' ten stroke segments. Only six 'tens' remained, sixty countable, seeable, do-able strokes. After two 'tens,' I still had a good lead, but from the corner of my eye I saw Biggy, in lane one, drawing closer. I wasn't so much slowing down, as he was speeding up. Didn't lactic acid burn his muscles? Didn't he tire like everyone else? Didn't he feel the pain?

I knew the answer.

Last 20 strokes: my eyesight tunneled into tight focus, like a telescope turned the wrong way. Nothing but pain now, seeming to emanate from every cell. Pain and still trying like hell to get across the line in first place.

Within the confines of the Lake Carnegie racecourse, my soul was tested in the final ten strokes. My body was sound. I offered the first 230 strokes as evidence. The last ten strokes would test my soul. The final question remained: Did I have the soul to stay ahead of Biggy?

I led by three feet, with Biggy surging closer on each stroke. I hated him in those last few seconds. He was the only reason my guts were being strewn over the water like an oil slick. Biggy and I were dead even, with one or maybe two strokes left.

I pressed one last time, and then looked toward the finish line flagman. The flag slashed down, and then up. The up stroke, identifying the second place finisher, was for me. Victory to John Biglow.

I stared into the green-brown water, watching my bloody soul drop through the depths, slowly rocking back and forth, occasionally glinting in the light, and then finally disappearing.

5

CAMP-BOUND
SUNDAY, MAY 6, CONCLUDED

AFTER SOME TIME I LIFTED MY FEET OUT OF THE FOOT-
stretchers, and hung my legs over the gunnels. The cool water
on my feet helped ease the pain. My body, right to the core,
felt badly overheated. Minutes passed before I took a stroke.

I found out later that a photograph had been taken of me
in this odd position, and the next day that photo was printed
in the *Los Angeles Times*. I could not imagine a more painful,
private time to be caught by the camera.

I vaguely thought that Tiff finished third, but I didn't know
the remaining order of finish. It didn't matter at the time.
Nothing mattered.

When I finally returned to the dock, Mitch told me he
was certain that I had won the race. But in this lowest of low
budget sports, we had no way to verify the finish because no
video camera was positioned on the finish line. I was
sentenced to live with the results for the rest of my life.

Every hour of my future, each challenge to come, had
depended on my crossing the finish line in first place. To lose

by a few inches - especially after having led by a big margin - made me sick from the inside out.

As part of the new drug testing procedure, immediately after the race the top three finishers from the trials were taken to the temporary USOC drug testing lab, set up in the Princeton Field House a few miles away. As Tiff and I deposited small quantities of urine into plastic cups, I thought over the possibilities.

The single scull had been the most straightforward method of making the U.S. Olympic rowing team. No camps, politics, or biased opinions affected the selection process. Two sculling boats remained to be decided: double and quad. As in the single scull, the Olympic representative for both these boats would be decided in trials. With a good partner, Tiff Wood for instance, we could prepare in solitude for the double trials.

Tiff said he could find a good boat for us to use and also a place for me to stay in Boston, where he lived. I was confident we could win the double trials without much trouble, and I was ready to shake hands on our partnership. Tiff was not so sure. "Nah," he said finally, "I don't think so. We'd be better off going to the camp."

Mitch and I went back to the Ramada Inn and packed our gear. I signed an $875 American Express tab for our room and meals. For this regatta, I spent slightly over $4,000 - a world record. Within an hour we were at Newark International Airport.

"Perhaps I'll go with you to L.A.," I said, thinking of the return ticket, still hot and fresh in my wallet. I had no taste for enduring another of Harry's camps, like the one I had experienced the previous summer in anticipation of the '83 Worlds. Far and away, the '83 camp had been the hardest training ordeal of my life. My rowing career had hung in the balance of every workout. Through luck, my strong back, and the injuries of other camp scullers, I had survived and made the team.

"You've nothing to gain by coming home," Mitch said. "I've no doubt Harry will put you and Tiff in the double. You'll probably have a great time at the camp. I suggest you give it your best shot 'cause it's a long way until the '88 Olympics."

'1988 Olympics.' A more virulent curse did not exist in my vocabulary. Simply put, I did not want to train another four years. Instead, I wanted to go backpacking, rent my own apartment, write a book, see the world, climb Mt. Everest, stay up late and watch David Letterman, start a new life. Start a real life. I was tired of constantly being tired, of feeling on the verge of getting ill, the usual physical state of being for any elite athlete. I wanted, needed, demanded my freedom. But even in my sorry state of mind, I knew I couldn't quit the fight without having solved this frustrating puzzle. To simply pack it in, to beg off, to go home and spend the rest of my life wondering why I had lost to Biggy on the last stroke, would be a lifelong torture. A special place in Hell is reserved for those athletes, in any sport, who lose in the last second of the race. I preferred not to join them. If my lower back and sanity were to remain intact, I had to concentrate my efforts on the only remaining alternative - Coach Harry's Camp.

I had been personally invited to Harry's camp by his assistant coach, Chris Allsopp, although my invitation was not particularly exclusive. Every sculler at the trials who had earned a place in the finals, plus 12 other scullers who had rowed with some distinction during the previous year, had also been invited.

A sculling camp could be exciting, even fun, or it could be pure torture, depending on your performance. With Harry Parker at the helm, I prayed for the best. Like all coaches, he had his favorites, and those favorites had their friends - all very complex and convoluted. Perhaps Mitch was right - I would have a good time at the camp. But then again, Mitch didn't know anything about sculling camps or Harry Parker.

Like a whirlpool, where the players struggled to stay afloat, over the next few weeks Coach Parker would pluck a few lucky survivors from out of the drowning depths and place them in the Olympic double or quad. I had no choice but to take a deep breath, suck it up, and jump in.

6

ENTER THE SPHINX
6:45 A.M., MONDAY, MAY 7, 1984

WALKING DOWN BOYLSTON STREET, I CAUGHT A GLIMPSE OF
the Harvard's Newell Boathouse, mirrored in the smooth, early
morning sheen of the Charles River. A dozen turrets and gables
enveloped the huge exterior, as though the builders had been
given plenty of wood and an unlimited amount of time to
complete their task. A wide dock, with a giant crimson 'H'
painted in the middle, led from the boat bays to the river's
edge. I doubt if this classic Ivy League scene had changed in
the last hundred years, nor was it likely to change for another
hundred.

A few minutes later, I stood on the deep boathouse porch
and pressed the doorbell. The front door of the Harvard Boathouse was always locked, and I would certainly never possess
a key. As I waited for the door to open, I thought about an
incident that had taken place inside the boathouse in 1980.
After practice one day, Harry suddenly marched up to me, his
face red with anger. He claimed that I had told two West
Coast rowers that they could keep their double scull in his
boathouse. My supposed audacity drove Harry insane, and

49

for five long minutes, he berated me in front of my rowing mates. Even now, years later, the memory of that verbal assault brings forth a nasty pain.

Harry's tirade was completely unjust in my opinion because I had never told these West Coasters anything of the sort. Eventually I learned that they had mentioned my name to Harry, thinking I had some influence with him, when actually I was only a marginal visitor at best. For the next two years, I had no dealings with Harry. In 1983 he coached the sculling team for the first time, and since I was a member of that team, we inevitably talked on occasion, although our conversations never strayed from the most superficial aspects of rowing.

I respected Harry's coaching ability, and at times I had desperately wanted him to bestow some modest praise on my shoulders. Now I simply tried to stay out of his way. To desire praise from Harry, I had gradually learned, was a waste of energy. Harry rarely offered even the slightest morsel of approbation. He asked nothing of me, nor of any oarsmen, except that I row as hard as possible. Year after year his lean coaching methods continued to work, as both his college and elite oarsmen won more than their share of races.

A Harvard oarsman unlocked the door, and I crossed the threshold. As I walked upstairs, I nodded to the straining oarsmen in a giant photo - the legendary '74 Harvard varsity crew. They were undefeated the whole year, except for the last race against the Russian National Team at the Henley Royal Regatta.

Deep grooves were cut into the wooden stairs from the heavy, post-workout trudging of countless oarsmen. These old stairs led straight to the heart of American rowing: the second floor of the Harvard boathouse. At the top of the landing was Harry's office - the heart of the heart of American rowing.

Inside the main room, I was relieved to see that Harry had not yet arrived. Few things annoyed Harry more than one of his oarsmen being late for practice. A dozen ergometers, the primary pastime of college rowers in the frozen winter, rested quietly in the middle of the room. I sat on one of the machines, but I didn't feel like rowing. My sore legs needed a few more days to recover from the single trials. I glanced around the room at the new banners and posters that had been acquired since my last visit a year ago. Banner stealing was a common pastime for college crews, and not surprisingly, Harvard had the best banner collection in the country.

My campmates were scattered around the room, about a dozen other men, all at least six feet tall, from 23 to 36 years old, conservative in appearance. The general shape of oarsmen, stocky, thick-legged, had not changed substantially since rowing was first introduced into the Olympics in 1896, nor probably for a thousand years before that. Taken together we looked like a heavyset, recreational basketball team, getting ready to play a crosstown rival.

Sculling attracts a very specific athlete. We are all college educated, and in many instances prep school and Ivy League educated. We often have a strong tradition of rowing within our families. We are much older than the Olympic contenders in such sports as gymnastics and swimming. Sculling skills require a long time to perfect. Some scullers practice a lifetime and yet seldom, if ever, take a good stroke.

Harry Parker had assembled a decent group of oarsmen. Almost all had rowed in last year's World Championships or in the less prestigious Pan American Games.

I nodded to Paul Enquist from Seattle, my double scull partner from last year. Next to Paul stood Casey Baker from Melbourne, Florida. I liked Casey. He surfed, which we had in common, and we had rowed together at the Worlds in 1977, my first full year of sculling. Bill Purdy, from Syracuse, sat on the floor next to the Philadelphia contingent of Jack Frackleton, Charlie Bracken, and Sean Colgan.

Next to Sean sat Ridgely Johnson, the giant Princeton man who always studied business textbooks when he wasn't rowing. Charlie Altekruse and Tiff Wood, both from Harvard, talked with Joe Bouscaren.

Big Jim Dietz, always boisterous and ready with a joke, sat next to the lightweight sculler Paul Fuchs. Both men trained at another ancient bastion of American rowing, the New York Athletic Club.

One sculler I did not recognize sat by himself. Eventually I learned his name was Gregg Montesi, a recent graduate of the Naval Academy.

All these scullers had their opinions of me, although I couldn't be certain where I stood with them, my contact having been too infrequent to develop any close friendships. One anonymous opinion of me was demonstrated in 1980. While training at the Harvard Boathouse, the name of my single scull, *Crippler*, was altered one night to read, *Crippled*. I spent the better part of my next morning's workout trying to decide if the revised name referred to my speed - slow - or to me, personally. The purpose and perpetrator of that modest crime are destined to be a mystery to the end.

If I hoped to survive this camp, I had to forget such cutting insults and assume a new attitude of mutual respect, pulling for the greater good and always speaking to my teammates in a manner so completely inoffensive that I would not upset even the most delicate sensibility. Rules to live by, summer sculling camp, 1984.

Until yesterday I had had little use for such attitudes, but now I needed them like the air I was breathing. Single sculling had made only the most straightforward demands on me. I had my boat, miles of open water, and my training partner, Dan Louis. Patience was a virtue that I did not need, nor had I cultivated patience as a hobby. Over the past year, I had worked myself into a massive ball of anger for the sole purpose of traversing the 2000-meter racecourse in a single scull faster than any American.

Time and circumstance had changed. I, too, had to change in order to match the new world. I would become a team player or I would be on the next plane home.

One last sculler, Bruce Beall, walked out of the bathroom. Most of the gossip, intimate team meetings, and other important fragments of rowing lore emanated from either the shower/bathroom facility or the locker room on the other side of the open floor. Since oarsmen traditionally made the walk from the locker room to the showers wearing only a towel slung over their shoulders, the whole upstairs portion of the Harvard boathouse was reserved exclusively for men.

Private men's club, health spa, old-fashioned bathhouse - the boathouse was all these things. On cold spring mornings, the steam flowed out the shower room windows like a house on fire. To stand naked with a bunch of other men in a white tile room, with 15 nozzles streaming hot water at full blast, was, I concluded after several summers, an acquired taste. Perhaps if I had attended boarding school, like so many of the scullers on our team, I would have been more comfortable in this chummy setting.

We were waiting for Coach Harry Parker, the patriarch of this domain.

Harvard Men's Varsity Crew and Coach Harry Parker, 21 years together, dozens of victories, including eighteen wins (against three losses) at the oldest intercollegiate sporting contest in the country, and Harvard's most important race of the season, the annual Harvard-Yale 'Four Miler.'

Harry had acquired a few nicknames along the way. My favorite was 'The Sphinx,' which perfectly described his regal posture and inscrutable demeanor as he drove the sleek Harvard coaching launch up the Charles River.

He owned every inch of the boathouse, from the crustaceans clinging to the underside of the dock to the lightning rod atop the highest pinnacle of the roof. His domain included the unpaved parking lot, the contents of every locker, the repair shop, the indoor rowing tanks. He also possessed a four-year lease on the soul of every Harvard oarsman who stepped across his threshold. Unlike many coaches, who incessantly screamed at their oarsmen, Harry spoke only rarely, relying instead on his pervasive aura to draw out the last, crucial ounce of fight within his men. One long, piercing look from Harry, and you shaped up fast.

Harry had watched me row for the first time in 1974. I was an excitable college sophomore attending a national team development camp in Hanover, New Hampshire. Throughout the camp, Harry said little to me, but when he spoke to the other rowers, or during the post-dinner meetings, I listened carefully. I was interested, not only in his words, but in learning how a champion sculler carried himself. Ten years later I concluded that Harry had changed little. I was different - stronger, tougher.

From down below I heard Coach Harry's booming voice calling any stray scullers upstairs. Good, let's get rolling.

As the meeting came to order, I joined a few other veterans toward the back of the red-rubber stretching mat. For a few moments, Harry said nothing as he carefully took stock of us, his new lads. At the same time, I studied him. He was wearing his favorite 60/40 parka, khaki pants, no hat. As usual, Harry looked trim, perhaps only five pounds heavier than his Olympic rowing weight. At the 1960 Rome Olympics, Harry had represented the U.S. in the single sculls, finishing in a respectable fifth place. Through the years he had never stopped training, and even now, he could often defeat his own oarsmen in such demanding athletic tests as running stadium stairs and racing his single scull in the Head of the Charles, a long distance race held every October. The 'Head,' in the opinion of most Cambridge oarsmen, ranked on par with the World Championships, perhaps even higher. Only the lines on his deeply weathered face, from squinting into the glare of the afternoon sun as he followed his beloved Harvard crews, showed his age. Harry Parker's true age? Timeless.

After a few standard lines of introduction, "We don't have much time, big task ahead, confident we can assemble two fast boats, essential we don't waste a single workout, pleased with what I saw at the single trials," Harry settled into the real business. "I'll have you work exclusively in doubles," he said. "The quads will stay on the trailer for the time being."

Excellent. Fine with me. As far as I was concerned, we could hammer the quads onto the trailer with 16-penny nails. Harry had implied that the double scull was his priority boat. He would put the top two scullers into the double, and the next best scullers into the quad. I wanted to row in the double, and since I prematurely considered myself the best sculler at the camp, based on the single trials, I smiled at the news.

Harry's next statement surprised me. "Each morning you'll row two 2000-meter races. The winning crew will stay together, and everyone else will be assigned a new partner. You'll use the afternoon practice to get acquainted."

This plan radically departed from Harry's time-honored selection method, known as seat racing. Seat racing consisted of a few, hotly contested mini-races, from two to five minutes in length, with several exchanges of personnel between boats within a workout. Using this method, a coach could quickly determine the fastest combination of scullers, although they might be the fastest for only a short distance rather than the 2000-meter Olympic distance.

I liked Harry's new strategy. Scullers with good endurance would probably dominate the races, rather than those who could grunt and pound away for a minute or two. I considered myself to be an endurance rower and definitely not a seat race sprinter.

Harry continued: "We're also going to break the squad into a Red Group and a Green Group. The Red Group will practice early, before breakfast, and the Green Group will train later in the morning. The Red Group will be made up of the quad and double from last summer's World Championships, plus Tiff, Ridgely, and Sean Colgan. Everyone else is in the Green Group."

Loosely translated, Harry meant the camp was breaking into a varsity squad and junior varsity squad, a good group and a not-too-good group, future Olympians and non-future Olympians. Since I had rowed in last year's double scull, I joined the varsity, instantly becoming the world's happiest camper. If I could stay alive for a few weeks, I was practically guaranteed a spot on the Olympic team.

Jim Dietz, a member of the newly formed junior varsity, did not like Harry's decision. Jim was the undisputed senior member of the squad, having been on countless national teams and three Olympic teams. Most recently he had made the finals at last week's single trials. Several members of the varsity had been unable to make the finals of the single trials, and this made Jim squirm with a sense of injustice. He believed that a good team boat sculler must also be competent in the single scull.

I'm sure other scullers in the room shared Jim's opinion, but unlike the rest of us, Jim wasn't afraid to speak up. In a surly tone, he asked Coach Harry: "When will the Green Group get a chance to break into the Red Group?"

"The two guys who show the most speed from the Green Group will get a shot at the Red Group," Harry replied, unmoved by Jim's insubordination. Jim would have his say in the end, but nothing could free him from the junior varsity.

In the final few minutes, Harry became sidetracked and launched into a sad soliloquy about the poor treatment he had received from the Men's Olympic Rowing Committee. Harry had requested to be named the supreme coach of the whole U.S. men's Olympic rowing team, both sweep and sculling. Without any explanation, his request had been flatly denied, and instead, he was offered the lowly sculling team.

The plum Harry wanted so passionately - coaching the men's Olympic eight-oared crew - had been awarded to Kris Korzenowski, a Polish man who came to the U.S. by way of Italy and Canada. Korzenowski was a unique man, a true coaching mercenary. All he needed was the right contract, three dozen big oarsmen, and the freedom to train his rowers without interference from anyone. Kris knew rowing like few men I'd ever met, especially the correct technique for moving a boat down the course at maximum speed. Many oarsmen found Kris' abrasive methods too critical, but because I dealt with him only rarely, I didn't mind his attitude. He had watched me row several times in Newport Beach and had given me a few good suggestions.

As the team meeting concluded, Coach Harry stared out the window at the quiet spring rain. The Charles River appeared like a fuzzy grey shadow. The bridge, the buildings across the way, the cars moving in slow motion along Memorial Drive, all seemed to be slipping in and out of a dull mist.

Harry appeared to be steeling himself against some unseen foe. Or perhaps he was simply trying to decide what to order for breakfast at the Mug and Muffin. Every day of his life, Harry earned another one of his nicknames, 'The Weird One.' Within a blink he was back with us, and he closed the meeting with a robust rendition of his favorite line: "Great day!"

After this chat we loaded the boat trailer with doubles, quads, an aluminum coaching launch, outboard engine, gas tanks, two dozen oars, slings, riggers. We were going camping in the countryside, Hanover, New Hampshire, the home of Dartmouth College.

The quad and double were both 'blind boats,' meaning we didn't have a coxswain to handle the steering. Rather than contend with the narrow, twisting, crowded Charles River, we needed New Hampshire's wide-open Connecticut River to stretch our water wings.

I was happy to be relocating. In my present state of mind, still disappointed from the single trials, I preferred Hanover's solitude to busy Cambridge.

7

WELCOME, MAKE YOURSELF UNCOMFORTABLE
MONDAY, MAY 7, CONTINUED

AT 4:00 P.M. WE STOOD OUTSIDE THE DARTMOUTH BOATHOUSE, a shack compared to the Harvard Boathouse, and listened to Coach Harry's final instructions.

"Listen bowmen," he warned. "There's lots of debris in the water so be extra careful. I don't want to start the camp with a couple of busted-up boats." Good advice, especially since Harry had assigned me to the bow position, making me responsible for steering the craft.

I liked rowing bow. The bowman had free license to look around, something I did no matter where I rowed.

The stroke man's job was to maintain the rhythm and rating, charging along through any-and-all distractions. The bowman, in addition to rowing in perfect unison with the stroke, must continually rotate his head like a beacon on a lighthouse, taking bearings on the shoreline, the opponents, making slight adjustments with his blades to keep the boat going straight down the course, watch for debris in the water, keep an eye on the coaching launch, and keep an eye on the stopwatch.

I had stroked my share of team boats, but when given a choice, I always preferred the bow.

I looked beyond Harry, towards the Connecticut River. The rain that had descended during this morning's team meeting in Cambridge had followed us to Hanover, and it appeared to be settling in for a long, long visit. Above the tree line, I saw an undeviating shade of flat grey stretching into the horizon, as though this color had been chosen to replace plain old blue.

Practicing in the steady rain was only a minor annoyance. Even without the rain, rowing is a wet sport, especially in team boats. My rowing technique included a healthy backsplash at the catch, which always insured that both the stroke and bowman would be soaked by the end of practice. A little rain simply filled in any remaining dry spots.

The real problem was cruising past the Dartmouth dock. Logs and branches, plastic bags, old tires, railroad ties, (which were the worst enemy because they barely showed above the surface of the water), scooted past. A good-sized chunk of wood, struck at full speed, could sink even the stoutest shell.

Harry had rented or borrowed a dozen double sculls to accommodate the unusually large number of scullers invited to his camp. Intentionally or not, by acquiring such a large number of boats, he had cornered the boat market and minimized the number of possible double scull challenges at the Olympic trials.

One of the boats Harry had borrowed was an exquisite, Swiss-made, wooden double scull, owned by Gail Cromwell, widow of the famous sculler, Sy Cromwell, who died of cancer in 1977. Sy won a silver medal in the double scull at the '68 Olympics, and his accomplishments inspired many young scullers, including Tiff Wood. Gail's double was the most beautiful boat on the trailer. The legendary Norwegian team of Frank and Alf Hansen had used this boat in their gold medal victory at the Montreal Olympics. The Cromwell double, at least in Gail's opinion, was still capable of winning an Olympic medal. Harry had personally assured Gail that her boat would be treated with the finest care at the camp.

Tiff Wood and Charlie Altekruse, both seasoned international scullers, were awarded the honor of rowing the Cromwell double this afternoon. They led the varsity squad upstream for the first of a thousand Connecticut River traversals. I followed Tiff's boat by a half-mile or so. This first row was for technique only, so I was relatively certain that Harry wouldn't come roaring up in his launch, demanding to know why I was so damn far behind the others. I had a knack for being slow off the dock, but I moved pretty fast on the flip side, especially if dinner was waiting.

My partner and I paddled easily around the first turn in the river. I craned my head, hoping to see another crew, but I saw nothing. Nor was Coach Harry in sight. Only the diminished wake from his launch, rebounding off the river-bank for the second or third time, acknowledged that he had passed this way.

Those ripples caressed the twisted, gnarled roots along the shoreline. The limbs of huge birch and pine trees hung over the river, shifting slightly in the afternoon breeze. If you're seeking a place of pure rowing beauty, I recommend the Connecticut River just above the town of Hanover.

Although my row was uneventful, the same luck didn't hold for Tiff and Charlie. "We were in the middle of our final power 20," Tiff told me later, "and then BAM! We smashed into a log or something. If Harry hadn't come alongside in his launch, we would have sunk in a minute." A foot-long gash, punched clean through the hull, put the Cromwell double out of action for the duration of the camp. I hoped this ruined boat did not in some way portend the future.

After dinner Tiff and I visited the Hell Hole Video Parlor, in downtown Hanover, for a couple of rounds of Centipede. The Hell Hole, a nickname I used, not knowing its real name, or if a name even existed, was behind Putnam's Drugstore, and down a gummy flight of stairs. Twenty video games were crammed into this cubbyhole, some new, using laser disc animation, and a couple of real antiques like Space Invaders. I pushed open the door, and we joined a dozen local teenagers and a few Dartmouth adventurers.

The Hell Hole's ambiance suited me well, as though it had been constructed especially for my use. Every video game started at zero, much like a rowing race, and then gradually the skilled and patient competitors forged ahead. For some players, a quarter lasted only 15 seconds, but for the experts, the same amount of money lasted long into the windowless night. Over the course of the camp, Tiff and I spent a small fortune at the Hell Hole, and not a penny was wasted.

I had known Tiff since the summer of 1977. At the '77 World trials, in our private single sculls, we waited at the starting line for the race to begin. At that moment, Tiff and I had only one thing in common - we were both rowing wooden shells, while almost everyone else was using the newer, fiberglass boats. Tiff and I raced dead-even, the whole 2000 meters, until the last five strokes. I managed to sneak ahead of Tiff by a foot and win the race, thereby earning a place in the finals. From that solitary day in the summer of 1977, I never defeated Tiff again until Sunday, May 6, 1984.

On the long row back to the Princeton boathouse, I introduced myself to Tiff, a nickname for Christopher.

We talked and laughed. I immediately liked him and we got along well.

We renewed our acquaintance each summer and finally, in 1980, we had a chance to row together, in the Olympic quadruple sculls. It was a great summer, except for President Carter's little boycott. Tiff and I had always stayed on good terms, and now, 1984, seven summers after we first met, I looked forward to rowing with him in the double scull for the first time. After our second and third place finishes at the Olympic single trials, I expected Coach Harry to immediately assign Tiff and me to the camp double.

Tiff was only slightly more enthusiastic than myself to be in Hanover. Incredibly, Tiff had gone from third in the single scull at the '83 Worlds, to first at last September's Pre-Olympic regatta, to third in our U.S. Olympic trials. Now he was relegated to the unending rigors of camp life, just like the rest of us.

Besides his rowing ability, Tiff had a blazingly fast, wickedly clever mind. At breakfast every morning, he inevitably solved all four Jumbles in the newspaper before I solved even one. He was a talented writer, primarily of semi-autobiographic, fully-pornographic short stories, and I always wondered why he didn't pursue his writing as more than a hobby. Tiff was tortured, no doubt, by the powerful demon that steered Harvard men to careers in banking or law or medicine. In Tiff's case, the demon had directed him to a career as an actuary.

I was free from the demon, and I said many prayers of thanks that I was not similarly tortured. My own job of the last three years had been arranged through the Olympic Job Opportunities Program, an excellent alternative to the East German student-soldier method of subsidizing athletes. I was a suit-wearing, tie-knotted, shoe-shined financial analyst at Wells Fargo Bank. With this job I could train at full-tilt, two workouts a day, while still earning a decent wage. I also learned a useful life lesson. Once the Olympics were over, I did not want to pursue a career in banking.

Most likely, I'd return to being a carpenter - rough framing to be exact. I had an affinity for building houses, as did several uncles and my grandfather. In this sport, the necessary pieces were a truckload of lumber, blueprints, a keg of nails, Skilsaw, tape measure, and the best tool ever invented in the history of mankind - a framing hammer. The fat, waffle-tipped head of my 32-ounce framing hammer drove home 16-penny nails with a single stroke. Included in the purchase was a correction key, the pointy hook on the end. A single scull and a framing hammer were remarkably similar: both were simple in design, and both responded quickly to their owner's personality.

I learned a lot of interesting facts on my way to earning two degrees at the University of California, Irvine, a Bachelor of Arts in Psychology and a Master's in Administration, Business. I received a different, perhaps more useful education from rough framing. I was fortunate to have the best instructor for framing, for life, for success - Carl Hilterbrand.

Carl framed a roof as though his life depended on it. He signed his name to every job. He worked alone on monster roofs, the kind that usually required a crew of five or six men. I loved working with Carl, but at the same time, I was more than a little afraid of him. If you saw Carl, huge, powerful arms and chest, black hair and beard, eyes like an animal kept too long in a cage, you'd know why.

For lunch he drank two 16-ounce cans of Coors beer, and then he walked along 2X6 joists turned on edge, full of knots and cracks, 30 feet above the ground, carrying a rain soaked 2X14 rafter. It was good therapy for Carl, and eventually it became good therapy for me.

I suppose you had to know him to appreciate him. He was hard in a way that had no place in our urban environment. He was violent from the inside out. He couldn't be around too many people. He had strength beyond belief. To him, every word and every action counted. Heaven and Hell crossed his path a dozen times a day. When a plumber accidentally let some water run onto our electrical cords, I believe I saw the pure primal man at his ultimate, angriest state. I learned a lot from Carl.

Carl and I were working on a roof in a big housing track when a young apprentice came around and said, "The inspector's here. Put down your guards."

"What's a guard?" I asked him. I had no idea a Skilsaw had a guard because Carl had taken the guards off his saws. In Carl's opinion, a saw guard was too dangerous. It made you sloppy, unaware of the madly spinning blade. You couldn't trust a saw guard. Better to work without a net, or a saw guard. The intensity was greater, more concentration, total commitment, better results.

I tried my best to apply that same attitude toward the single trials. I had raced without a safety net, no team boats, no camp, no tomorrow. Win or die trying.

"You don't ever want to feel too good," he told me a few days before we parted company. For a long time, I didn't know what he meant, but after a month at the camp I knew exactly the meaning of his words.

Every day at camp, for at least a moment or two, I thought of Carl Hilterbrand.

8

INCREASING UNEASINESS
MAY 8, 1984

WE RACED THE NEXT MORNING. I CAN'T REMEMBER WHO WON our maiden double scull race, but I clearly remember that my boat finished lengths behind. My partner was Bill Purdy, a future dentist who had rowed in last year's quad at the World Championships. He was a fair sculler, actually quite good considering he was a sweep convert from the '80 Olympic eight-oared shell. I figured he'd eventually find a place in this year's Olympic quad.

If I had been training on my own, I could have told you everything about those races. I always kept a detailed practice log, noting my opponents, whether I won or lost, the margins and ratings and times, even little details like tide and weather conditions, noting everything about every piece.

The word 'piece' is used in rowing to denote a single unit of time or distance. For instance, a common workout, six times 500 meters, is made up of six pieces, each 500 meters long.

My entries leading up to the trials had been tightly written, frantic messages about the work I'd just completed, and the way I was going to convert that work into speed, and then use that speed to propel me to victory at the trials. The day after the trials, the page was blank. Under Harry's wing I lost all interest in maintaining my diary. He was in charge of keeping those facts, and I had no doubt that he was doing a fine job. How strange, I thought, that at this rowing camp, where I had all the time in the world to write careful journal entries, I completely abandoned the practice.

When training alone, my favorite book was my training journal. At home, in the top drawer of my dresser, I had a stack of such journals, one for every year, a veritable *Encyclopedia of Rowing* by Brad Lewis.

This year I was using a thick three-ring Wells Fargo notebook, the better to add more pages, and it appeared more businesslike on my desk. Taped to the inside front cover, in two-inch-high letters, were the words: PROVE YOU'RE TOUGH. For the back of my book, I borrowed the cover of a recent issue of *Rowing U.S.A.* The picture caught Tiff Wood in mid-stroke, winning the Head of the Charles regatta. All year I had been focusing on Tiff as my main competition at the single trials. Too bad I had underestimated Biggy, although I don't know what changes I would have made in my preparations, or in the race.

Taped to an inside page was a quote from a medical journal: "Testosterone is a potent steroid used by athletes in weight events, football, and bodybuilding. One side effect is aggressive behavior by users." Thanks to a welcome fluke of nature, I possessed the most important effect of steroids - aggressive behavior - without having to take the drug.

Aggressive behavior is rarely condoned in our civilized paradise, except in sports, and my sport of choice was rowing. Thus I could, and did, take exception to the 'no aggressive behavior' rule. Rowing wasn't a hobby for me, nor a dilettante's pastime, nor a rich man's sport, nor a spoiled boy's game. I approached rowing with the utmost seriousness. Unfortunately, I wasn't innately gifted with exceptional strength or endurance. I had no choice but to practice hard and obsessively, always driven by an underlying aggression.

A magazine advertisement for Bankers Trust Company showed a man climbing the sheer face of Yosemite's El Capitan with the phrase, "Excellence is achieved only through consistency and innovation. And drive." Good words to live by for a free thinking sculler.

My Mom hand-lettered this message on a 3X5 card: "The harder you work, the luckier you get." My beautiful Mom.

A picture of Sid Vicious cut from *Penthouse Magazine* provided me with fine inspiration. Sid, of the punk rock group, The Sex Pistols, was on stage, shirtless, his face busted open, blood flowing down his chest. As a singer, he was nothing. As a guitarist, he was less than nothing. Despite his lack of talent, Sid drove people wild with his performances. Only one thing mattered - his intense spirit - and it shone through with crystal clarity. One song in particular, *Sub-mission*, had the primal, unrelenting rhythm that I sought when I raced. As part of my pre-race ritual, I always funneled *Sub-mission* two or three times through my Walkman, directly into my psyche. Both The Sex Pistols and Sid Vicious have since retired from competition.

With each daily entry, and with the addition of each new clipping, I was writing the book on my rowing experience, or more accurately, the book on myself. Almost every champion has something to say, and I liberally drew inspiring messages from *Playboy, People, Sport in the GDR*, (I was one of the few U.S. subscribers), the *Los Angeles Times, Decathlon Challenge* by Bruce Jenner, *Velo News, Rolling Stone, and Peak Performance* by

Charlie Garfield. They all share a common theme: the celebration of pure, aggressive, animal energy. Count me in.

After breakfast, I sought out Harry's assistant coach, Chris Allsopp, to have a little chat. I had two very important requests. I wanted to be in the double scull, as opposed to the quad, and I wanted to row with Tiff Wood. I saw no reason to waste any more time trying different combinations. Let the Lewis-Wood double scull quickly prove its superiority, and then allow us to start training for the trials and the Games.

Naturally, I would have preferred to talk directly to Harry, but I knew he didn't appreciate his oarsmen giving him coaching advice. I prided myself on my toughness, but in this arena - directly telling Harry of my frustrations - I was remarkably wimpy. Too bad. I might have saved us a lot of trouble.

Harry and me. I saw Harry as part father, part God's Moses, part Melville's Ahab. Harry had been a champion, never a gold medalist, but still one of the best in the world, and he was still remarkably tough. He was wilder than I, always diving off the highest ledge when we went to the local swimming hole. Harry was probably the only man in the world who could make me question my own abilities.

Chris Allsopp afforded the second best audience. I had met Chris six years ago, during the winter of 1977-78. He was already an international sculling veteran, having rowed on a half-dozen junior and national teams. At that time I was at the exact opposite end of the spectrum. After nearly destroying my right leg, I was struggling to get back into shape.

Three years later, Allsopp and I became quad mates on the 1980 Olympic Team. He stroked the boat, while I rowed in the two seat, with Tiff between us. Tom Howes was in the bow. Where is Tom now? Fat and happy, I hope.

Chris and I expended gallons of sweat that summer, racing on the East coast and in Europe. We shared the team van and hotel rooms. I ate a score of meals with him, but we never became friends. I was still a lowly, struggling sculler, trying to secure my membership in the exclusive national team club. Now, summer of '84, assistant coach Chris Allsopp once again had the superior position.

When most of the others scullers had left the dining hall, I put my tray on the table in front of Allsopp and sat down directly across from him. "You must be feeling awful good," I said. "You and Harry and Biggy are the only three guys on the Olympic Team."

"Well, to be honest, I think I'd feel better if I was still rowing," Chris said.

Allsopp resumed eating his Rice Krispies, so I leaned a little closer: "I talked to Tiff last night," I said, "and we were hoping to get a chance to row the double together." Chris looked amused as I continued my plea. "One practice is already wasted, and we don't have much time. I know Tiff and I will be the best combination, but we should start practicing now, before we get too far into the camp."

"Well, I'll be sure to tell Harry," Chris said, with a laugh.

Rowing in the quadruple scull, in my opinion, was the sporting equivalent of working in a factory, especially the middle two seats, where I would probably be placed. In a quad, the stroke set the rhythm and the bowman performed the steering duties. I was too big for the bow seat, and I lacked the rhythm of a good stroke. My strength was best suited to the number two or three seats, where I would be asked to keep quiet as a mouse and pull until my legs fell off.

I could tolerate laboring in this blast furnace - it was certainly better than not making the team - if I had three good mates with whom to share my burden. Unfortunately, the quality of scullers in this country dropped off rather quickly after the first four or five men; and the camp's two best rowers were already destined for the double scull.

Regardless of the men Harry selected to fill the seats, his quad was expected to have an easy time in winning the Olympic trials. One or two opposing quads might make the short trip to Princeton from Philadelphia. Perhaps a pick-up boat would drive down from Boston. I expected something similar to the 1980 Olympic quad trials, where my boat won by 43 seconds.

The Olympics would not be so easy. The East Germans, West Germans, Canadians, and Russians all had fast quads. The same four men had been rowing in the West German quad, the reigning World Champions, since 1979. All these crews had the basic ingredients - coaching, equipment, talented scullers - plus they had years of racing experience. Against such tough opposition, Harry's quad would be hard pressed to make the Olympic finals, much less win a medal.

The double scull was a different, far better story. A double responded immediately to the spirit of the scullers. Two aggressive men like Tiff and me, for instance, could make a double scull fly down the course.

A tiny ego factor also entered the picture. A quad rower - no matter how good - was virtually anonymous, while champion double scullers could achieve some notoriety.

Students of international rowing can recite the names of the world's best double scullers: Norway's Hansen Brothers, Switzerland's Studach and Burgin, and East Germany's Heppner and Lange. I wanted my name on that list. I could no longer achieve the ultimate fame, the single scull, but I would settle for the double.

9

YOU CAN'T ROW AND HOPE
MAY 19, 1984

LIKE THE SIX PREVIOUS ROWING CAMPS I HAD ATTENDED, this newest edition lurched and lumbered through the first days. The quality of rowing was adequate in the beginning, but soon drifted to the lowest common denominator.

Scullers slammed into the catch, grunted and pounded out the drive, and then zipped up the slide to the catch once again with total abandon. Boats nearly collided, oars overlapped, bowmen steered in front of other boats to wake them down. All wonderfully amusing, if you were winning. Harry had his hands full, simply making sure we didn't stray into the bank at the narrowest part of the river. One morning Harry became furious that the bowmen were not looking ahead as often as he demanded. He shouted out a line, a Harry classic, which will bring a smile to the face of any sculler who was on the river at the time. "You can't row and hope." Row and hope. All we did was row and hope.

All wounds were healed in the Dartmouth dining hall, which faithfully lived up to its reputation as serving the best training food in the northeast. The three-flavor soft ice cream machine, looked upon as a shrine by visiting oarsmen, worked overtime after every meal to cool the camp's overheated oarsmen. During my summers in Dartmouth, I had perfected the root beer/soft vanilla ice cream float, and after two or three helpings, I didn't care about anything.

Many of the camp warriors made nightly treks from our residence, the Chieftain Motel, a few miles outside of town, to Peter Coffin's Bar, one of the livelier places in Hanover. In this all-green college town, a man could still impress a female student by telling her that he was trying out for the Olympic team. I rarely went out with the other scullers. In retrospect, this was probably not wise. If I had made an effort to be friendlier with my campmates, perhaps I would have had an easier time when teamed with them.

Going from solitary sculler to cooperative team player was proving more difficult than I had imagined. I had derived much pleasure in taking responsibility for my single scull training and racing. Those days were long gone. I missed them, especially after a few days when my performance at the camp began to turn into a floating disaster. I lost race after race, and my standing in the Varsity soon fell to the bottom of the squad. Regardless of my partner, I usually performed adequately on the first race, and then lost the second race by a big margin. I was suffering from a textbook case of inconsistent effort.

More than any rowing fault, Harry despised inconsistency. It showed weakness of character, faulty conditioning, inadequate concentration, a lack of toughness. But this new mantle felt wrong on my head. All year I had made a special effort to be consistent in my training, a good, steady, powerful sculler, capable of performing under any conditions, no matter how tired. Times had changed or I had changed. Something was definitely wrong.

I'd spent hours trying to figure out exactly what it was, but to no avail. In exactly two weeks, I had managed to row myself into a tight corner. Harry planned to cut about half the scullers in a few days. Now I was on the verge of setting a rowing precedent: finishing second in the single trials to being cut from the sculling camp in the first round.

As I left the dining hall, I was pulled aside by Chris Allsopp and given more bad news. He told me to expect a visit that afternoon from our head coach.

No torture could be worse, I soon learned, than waiting for Harry Parker. Even when diffused among a dozen teammates, his Sphinx-like presence was barely tolerable. A close quartered, one-on-one confrontation was almost too heady to imagine. While waiting in my motel room, I tried in vain to remember even one instance when Harry and I had talked alone. My roommate, a tough lightweight named Paul Fuchs, was reading a book on the bed next to mine. I had neglected to tell Paul of Harry's impending visit. I wanted Paul's company until the last possible moment.

I was trying to concentrate on *Family Feud* when the expected knock echoed through the door. "Got a minute?" Harry asked. I felt like asking Harry to come back after *Family Feud*, but thought again, knowing his unpredictable sense of humor. I leaped from the bed, turned off the television and said, "Sure, come on in. Chris told me to expect you."

"Right. Well, this won't take long," Harry said. "Say Paul, can you leave us for a minute?" Paul Fuchs was already tying his shoes, and a second later, he sprinted out the door.

"So," I asked, taking the offensive, "what's on your mind?"

"Well, what's on your mind is a more timely question," Harry countered. "You don't seem to have much concentration when you're racing. Several of your partners have talked to me about you having a bad attitude. I have a feeling this attitude is preventing you from winning your share of races."

"Oh, okay, hmmm." I didn't know what to say. Bad attitude, B.A., B.A. Lewis, B.A. Baracus, Mr. T, *The A Team*, starring George Peppard, who had starred in a television series called *Banachek*, where the opening credits showed a single sculler rowing up the Charles River, only it had been a stand-in because George couldn't row, and the close-up had been shot in a studio on a rowing machine, and once when I was rowing in 1977, or was it 1982, a guy called out from the shore, "Hey Banachek." I doubted if Harry would care to float down my winding stream of consciousness.

He hadn't asked me any direct questions, but I felt as though I should say something, if only to prove that I was paying attention. I said, "Yeah."

I hoped he was wrong. But maybe he was right. He was definitely right about one point: I wasn't winning my share of races. I sat stock still, waiting for the next revelation.

We talked a few minutes, and then Harry made the closing statement I had been anticipating. "I don't like to say this," he said, "but if you don't show some signs of improving - very quickly - you're going to be cut from the squad. To put it bluntly, you either win tomorrow or you're gone." Harry stood up and left without another word.

What the hell, I thought, I didn't want to sleep tonight. I'll just sit here and contemplate my impending date with Charlie Altekruse, my partner for tomorrow's race, and my newfound enemy.

During the afternoon practice, Charlie and I had endured a miserable row, fighting each other up and down the Connecticut River. Our technique had been adequate, but from the first stroke, we simply did not cooperate. If humanly possible, Charlie and I would have pulled the boat apart and gone our separate ways.

Charlie and I had been on friendly terms last summer at the '83 World Championships. He had rowed in the three seat of the quad, behind stroke man John Biglow. Their quad, with Joe Bouscaren in the bow and Bill Purdy in the two seat, had been expected to challenge for a medal, but it failed to make the finals.

Charlie and I talked quite often during the summer, and as I remember, we parted on good terms. Yet from the very first hour of the '84 sculling camp, a strong and mutual dislike had developed between us. Even as we unloaded the boats from the trailer, Charlie had accused me of laziness, saying "Come on, Lewis, you can't be hanging back while we're doing all the work. Get with the program." Perhaps I should have confronted him right on the spot and found out what the hell was going on. Instead, I did nothing. The source of our personal antagonism was to remain a mystery to me, although I have a feeling he simply needed a target for his frustration. For Charlie, I was the perfect target.

Only the day before Charlie had shouted at me as I left for the Dartmouth weight room, "You might win a few races if you spent less time lifting weights." Perhaps he was right, but at least I wasn't losing my strength, a common occurrence during long stretches of uninterrupted hard rowing, such as we were enduring.

With my life on the line in nine hours, I hoped Charlie was sleeping well, getting lots of rest, and having good dreams.

10

ODE TO JIM DIETZ
MAY 20, 1984

"HEY CHARLIE," I SAID, AS WE PADDLED TOWARDS THE START-
ing line, "how 'bout if we kick some ass today?"

"Sure," Charlie said. "I'm up for that."

I was rowing in the bow seat, and although I heard his
reply, I was unable to see his facial expression. His words had
a flat, neutral tone, neither enthusiastic nor sarcastic. I needed
to see his face before I could judge his sincerity.

Five minutes later, we bolted off the starting line and
opened up a two-length lead. But instead of adding to our
lead, we cruised the last half of the race, thus allowing the
other boats to crawl up our stern. We won, but our final
margin of victory was only one boat length. Instantly, I felt
Harry's gaze on me. Charlie and I had to win the next race, or
I'd be on my way home.

"Nice rowing, Charlie," I said during the few minutes rest
between races. "Let's make it two for two." Charlie didn't
answer this time. Okay, no problem, I thought, don't say a
word if you're not in the mood.

Can two rowers who don't get along win a boat race? Between pieces I spent a few seconds contemplating this question. Charlie and I had just won a race, and we didn't care much for each other. But this was small time racing. How about at the World Championship level? Some rowers I knew believed that their job was simply to tug on the oars for six or seven minutes until they crossed the finish line. Other rowers believed that an interpersonal awareness seminar should take place between the 500 and 1500 meter marks. I agreed more with this latter notion. A lot more went into winning than simply tugging on the oars - the spirit of the oarsmen was all important. Maybe Charlie and I could fake it for one more piece.

After a shaky start on the second race, fumbling for a few strokes, and then veering off course in the process, which was my fault since I was steering, we trailed the lead double by one length at the halfway mark. Over the next 500 meters, instead of catching up we fell a little further behind. Without looking toward the coaching launch, I could feel Coach Harry's stare burning a hole in my shirt. "Take it up two," I said to Charlie. I managed only a whisper, and I was unsure if he heard me.

Taking up the rating is not always the solution to turning around a losing piece. At some point, the rating cannot go any higher without causing the stroke to shorten, but our rating was two or three beats below the other boats, and time was running out.

Perhaps Charlie was distracted or too tired, but regardless of the reason, our rating didn't budge. I said again, "Take it up." Only one length separated us from the lead boat, and we had thirty seconds to go. If we pulled even - forget winning at this point - I wouldn't look too bad. With ten strokes to go, we trailed the lead boat by only a few feet and we were moving on them. Our rating finally went up one or two beats, and we finished within a seat of the winners. A tie, I told myself.

I was exhausted as we crossed the line, while almost immediately I heard Charlie chatting to Joe Bouscaren in the next boat. I couldn't have said my own name for at least a minute. At the moment I didn't care. Talk away - maybe he was in super shape, with energy to spare. Our efforts had earned me a reprieve - good enough. Now let's get back to the dock.

As promised, Coach Harry eliminated six scullers after the morning practice. He was unusually gentle in administering the cleaving knife, visiting each man in his room and explaining why his services were no longer needed. As expected, all the junior varsity scullers, with the exception of two men, Jack Frackleton and Charlie Bracken, were given their walking papers.

I had known both sides of the equation. At my first and only national team sweep camp in 1975, the coach posted a list of survivors. The oarsmen whose names were not on the list had to vacate their rooms by sunset. My name had been omitted, overlooked, a mistake perhaps, and I remember standing in front of the list for ten minutes, willing my name to appear.

I gave most of our departing scullers a wide berth, although to my closest comrades I offered a few words, "Next time, Fuchs," "We both know you got screwed, Casey. What did you expect from Harry?" My words sounded condescending, and I wished I had said nothing. Every departing sculler took a bit of the camp with him, and for some reason, the less proficient scullers - the first to be cut - were the most fun to have around.

Not surprisingly, Harry cut Jim Dietz. Rather than take the news in stoic silence, so typical of rowers, Jim departed in a blaze of glory. I was watching *The Price is Right*, when I heard a commotion in the Chieftain's west wing, where Harry and Allsopp had their room. Along with the rest of the team, I ran toward the noise. Jim had marched into Harry's room, and was verbally blasting away with both barrels, telling Harry exactly where to stick his megaphone. Harry was all tensed up, as if waiting for Jim to take a swing at him, but only harsh words about prejudice and favoritism pummeled Harry.

Jim's parting words achieved instant cult status in the rowing world. Following a gush of obscenities, he boomed: "You don't know shit about rowing, and even less about people."

Without waiting for a reply, Jim turned, marched to his car, and screeched away from the Chieftain, throwing gravel onto the balcony of the second floor. His parting words had spoken for every man who had been cut, and perhaps for a few of us who survived.

Ten scullers remained after the dust settled. Each one of us, especially me, was thankful that Harry was also leaving. He was needed in Cambridge to prepare his college crew for the Harvard-Yale 'Four Miler.' Our camp had already consumed two precious weeks, and yet only six scullers had been trimmed from the squad - a frustrating, meager accomplishment. Even worse, I had yet to row with Tiff.

Chris Allsopp had been left in charge, and I assumed he was merely our babysitter, without any real authority to make decisions. Harry had probably told him to simply keep us out of mischief.

Coach Harry promised to reappear in two weeks, make the final cuts, and then establish the boatings for our first race, the Lucerne International Regatta in Switzerland. We would be racing a quad and two double sculls in Lucerne - eight scullers altogether. Two more men would be cut - Ridgely and Paul, or Jack and Paul, or maybe Bracken and Ridgely. I still had a good chance, at least to make the Lucerne trip. I'd survived the first cut, which was all I cared about. With a few days rest, away from Harry, with more soft ice cream, I'd soon be on the right track.

The Lucerne Regatta would be our best, perhaps our only legitimate test of speed prior to the Olympics. For the rowers of some European countries, Lucerne served as their Olympic trials. If they failed to do well, they would not be sent to the Games. Following the usual international custom, a self-contained regatta was to be held on Saturday, followed by another self-contained regatta on Sunday. Preliminary heats would be held each morning, with finals in the afternoon.

Professional basketball players battle through 88 regular season games. Baseball teams play 166 games. Yet for all our months of preparation, our total racing season, after the single trials, consisted of only three regattas - Lucerne, the double or quad trials, and the Olympics.

While I napped, a steady, hard, undeviating rain began to fall. Perhaps Jim Dietz had cast some rain-inducing curse on us while driving back to New York. The rain we had endured the first few days of camp was a light mist compared to the chunky drops that clattered on the Chieftain's aluminum roof. On the first rainy day, the local television news discussed the change in weather: "Expect more rain in the Hanover region." By the third day, the heavy rains made the regional newscasts: "Some minor flooding in Hanover." On the fifth day, the raging Connecticut River was national news: "Record flooding in New Hampshire."

Huge, slow moving islands of debris floated down the river toward the dam, chased by never-ending whirlpools. After three days, when rowing became impossible, Tiff and I donned our rain gear, and drove to a nearby dam to watch the wreckage. We joined a crowd of about 50 people and screamed our delight as tons of floating junk cascaded over the dam. The loudest cheers were for whole trees, huge and full of spring leaves, that reluctantly tumbled over the precipice. The trees would emerge at the base of the dam a half-minute later, stripped of every leaf, as if they had passed through a king-sized Cuisinart.

11

OVERDOSE OF FRENCH SLEEPING PILLS
JUNE 1, 1984

DURING HARRY'S ABSENCE THE URGENCY OF OUR ROWING
slackened, and I began to feel terminally bored. My daily naps,
a tradition at rowing camp, lengthened from an hour's
duration, to two hours, to three-hour sleep marathons.

I tried to resist naptime's luxurious narcotic by inventing
jobs. First, I bought some pre-recorded audio tapes and
attempted to learn French, the great language of rowing. As
decreed by the supreme governing body of international rowing, FISA, Fédération Internationale des Sociétés d'Aviron,
every command given by the officials on the racecourse must
be spoken in French. I already knew the main words:

Cinq minutes - Five minutes until the start

Faux depart - False start

Etes vous prêt? - Are you ready?

Partez - Start

I attempted to learn my French in bed, which was a
mistake since I always gave in to the call of the nap. Napping
and soft ice cream were now firmly established as the only
highlights of my day.

Just before Harry left for Boston, Mitch Lewis arrived in Hanover to try out for the position of team trainer. Although I refrained from telling anyone, I paid for Mitch's roundtrip flight from Los Angeles, and I also paid him a salary of $300 a week while he stayed in Hanover.

In 1983 several of our scullers had suffered from lower back problems, and so I knew our team desperately needed Mitch's services. Mitch was capable of fixing broken scullers. He knew massage and chiropractic techniques. He could align your back and sync-up the hemispheres of your brain. His bag of tricks was deeper than any I had seen. We needed him.

With Mitch on our team, I hoped to break new ground. Traditionally, U.S. rowers did not use trainers, masseurs, chiropractors, or sports psychologists. My inspiration came from the East Germans, whom I had seen being massaged at the '83 Worlds. The Easties came to win, no holds barred. They were champions. I wanted to be a champion.

I had hoped that Mitch would prove his value to Harry and the other scullers during his stay in Hanover, but all he managed to do was spot me on a few squats in the Dartmouth weight room. A trust between athlete and trainer, especially a trainer as unconventional as Mitch, takes months to form. We had only two weeks. Despite the cool reception he received from the other rowers, my trust in Mitch was not lessened. I promised him a share of my Olympic gear, if, through some miracle, I made the team.

By imitating the Easties in hiring a trainer, I was being true to my premiere rule in rowing - do whatever it takes to become the best sculler in the world. This rule encouraged unlimited use of expensive video equipment, massage therapy, steam saunas every Thursday, and especially, the services of the best trainer I could find. 'Whatever it takes' must always take the form of proper, positive, legal, drug-free behavior. Maintaining integrity is all important.

But much like my rowing journal, so far at the camp I had put away my 'whatever it takes' rule. I'd shut off that part of my being and left all responsibility to Harry, who happened to be out of town at the moment. The 'whatever it takes' rule works best, I decided, when you take complete responsibility for all aspects of your training.

The Chieftain's only pay phone was a rotary dial antique, set into a little booth next to the check-in desk. I impatiently waited my turn behind the other scullers for the privilege of reestablishing contact with the outside world. I called home to make sure I was still loved, my bills weren't overdue, and my girlfriend was suitably lonely. I needed to know that life beyond the borders of Hanover was still worth living. The pay phone provided the sole link to my friends and family, the greatest entities on earth.

While waiting to use the phone, I occasionally talked to my old partner, Paul Enquist. Somehow Paul had managed to slip even further down on Harry's scale. I was holding down the number eight position, with Paul at number nine. The lowest rung, number ten, belonged to Ridgely Johnson. We would have talked more often, Paul and I, except we had little to say. Last season had not ended on a positive note. Now we had a harder task ahead of us, and last year's partnership was of little help.

We had been given one chance to prove ourselves in the double scull at the camp, and when that day arrived, we were both overdue for a win. I was certain that Paul and I would put the reigning camp champions, Charlie Altekruse and Joe Bouscaren, into their rightful places - as quad rowers. Unfortunately, Paul and I started slowly on each of the two races.

We struggled to within striking range of Charlie and Joe at the finish, gaining on them with each stroke, climbing up their stern, hauling them down, but each time we crossed the finish line a half-boat behind.

"A loss is a loss," Charlie reminded us as we paddled back to the boathouse. Charlie and Joe had been teamed together in the first few weeks at Hanover, and they had won with enviable regularity. Barring a serious accident, they were clearly on their way to being the new camp double.

Paul Enquist was 28-years old, balding, very tall, with long arms that gave him a huge reach in the boat. Usually he wore a white baseball cap to hold the sun at bay. When tested at the rowing camp, only one other sculler had a higher percentage of body fat than Paul - me. High body fat is not usually associated with champion scullers. Of the hundreds of college rowing teams in the U.S., Paul's alma mater, Washington State University, was perhaps furthest from being termed a rowing power. Last summer, after six years of trying, Paul had made his first national team.

His father, a salmon fisherman out of Seattle, was looking forward to retiring, and Paul was looking forward to taking over the business. To many people, Paul did not exude the killer instinct so often associated with champion athletes. But after spending the previous summer with him, I knew that he possessed the passion, the necessary spark, to uncork some amazing performances. I don't know the genesis of his spark, but I knew he had it, and I knew it could burn brightly.

With 500 meters to go in the semi-final race of the '83 Worlds, Paul and I rumbled past the Soviets, and then, on the last stroke, we nudged ahead of the Canadians. Dramatic, gutsy rowing. We rowed down that 2000-meter course in 6:17, three seconds behind the winning East Germans. Generally, a 2000-meter time is not significant because variables such as wind and water conditions change from hour to hour. Still, 6:17 for 2000 meters in a double scull, under any conditions, was exceptionally fast. The East Germans eventually won the Worlds, while we finished dead last, having raced a very poor final. We should have won a medal.

Paul's father had little interest in rowing or the Olympics, but his mother gave him unbridled support. Salmon fishing, his mother, his girlfriend (a candidate for the women's sculling team), and plain, hard rowing comprised the essence of this humble man.

So far, the best camp double was clearly Charlie and Joe, but Tiff and I were still prepared to tear them to shreds in the final few days. All we needed was a nod from Coach Harry, although I was beginning to lose hope that we would receive the coveted nod. Perhaps Harry was holding back his trump card, Tiff and Lewis, until he returned from Boston. Tiff was surprisingly indifferent to our not having been given a chance to row together - he was holding his own in the races, several notches above me, and I suppose he was content to let things ride.

Still, Coach Harry's lack of experimentation didn't make sense. Why keep apart the second and third best scullers in the country, a ranking I still believed, although it was based on long outdated results from the single trials. Only Harry Parker knew what the hell was going on, and he was still a few hundred miles away.

Harry's return was now two days overdue, and with the Lucerne Regatta drawing near, selection time was almost over. During his absence we had replaced the raging Connecticut River with a new practice site: Goose Pond, the secret nesting ground for the entire mosquito population of the vast northeast.

12

CALIGULA, UNCUT, UNEDITED
JUNE 5, 1984

I SAT WITH THE REST OF THE TEAM ON THE CROWDED FLOOR in Tiff's room, watching the uncut version of the movie *Caligula*. The cramped room was alive with cheers and advice for the actors, as we replayed a sex scene two or three times - typical camp anti-boredom stuff. Suddenly Coach Harry appeared in the doorway.

His presence instantly reduced us to silence, as if our volume control knobs had been turned to zero. We sat still, waiting for some words, insults, pep talk, "Good movie, I've seen it twice," something from the mouth of the Sphinx to break the tension. Finally, Coach Harry cleared his throat and said, "Let's turn that off. I want to outline the work we have ahead of us in the next three days."

Our fabled leader looked tired. His white-hot magnetism, which had driven young men, me included, to the limits of physical exhaustion, seemed to have cooled to its lowest ebb. No doubt his team's loss to Yale in the Four Miler a few days earlier didn't help matters.

"Based on the results from earlier racing and Chris' obser-vations," Coach Harry said, "the camp double will be Charlie and Joe. That leaves us six practices to find the fastest combination for the quad. Tomorrow afternoon we'll start seat racing to determine the four guys who'll fill those seats. Be prepared to give it everything you have."

Bad news. So much for the Lewis-Tiff double scull com-bination, and so much for Allsopp only being our babysitter.

"Also," Coach Harry said, "I want to see Ridgely and Paul for a few minutes." He glanced at the television as if to say, now you can go back to your masturbatory fantasies. Then he left the room.

Ridgely and Paul slowly rose from their niches, and without a word they cautiously picked their way through the stretched-out bodies on the floor. The rest of us stared in embarrassed silence at the television. My old partner, one-half of last year's sixth fastest double scull team in the world, was about to be released from bondage.

A few minutes later, I sought out my old partner. Yes, Harry's parting message had been succinct, and now Paul was sitting by himself in his room, knitting the last few rows of a ski hat, his fourth of the camp.

"So, the news is bad, eh?" I said, not sure how to approach this sad fisherman.

"I knew it was coming," Paul said. "My Mom is really going to be unhappy." These words showed the true Paul. His concern was for his mother's feelings and not his own.

"Listen, Paul. I wouldn't be too hasty to head back to Seattle if I were you."

Paul looked up from his knitting for the first time. "What would you do in my situation?" he asked.

"I'd stick around a few days. If not here, perhaps in Boston. Keep training, but don't be in a hurry to hook up with a partner until you see what happens in the next few days."

He put down his knitting and said, "Might you be interested in rowing the double with me?"

I had hoped that Paul would not ask this question, but since he had my only choice was to avoid answering it directly.

"Listen, Paul," I said. "You're on the outside looking in, and I know it doesn't feel good. You're locked out. I've been there myself on many occasions. But sometimes it's better to be on the outside. You have more freedom to do what you think is best. Take me for instance. I'm on the inside, but I have no control. If Harry decides I'm not good enough for the quad, then I'll be forced to row in the camp's second double. I'd rather row with you at the double trials than play that game."

Paul was giving me his full attention by this time.

"Stick around for a few days," I continued, "or if you leave Hanover, let me know where I can reach you. If Harry gives me the shaft, then we'll row the double. I'm sure we can beat Charlie and Joe in a legitimate 2000-meter race. It'd be wild, eh?"

"Sure, I'll stick around," he said, resuming his knitting. "Why not? Salmon season doesn't open for another month."

I left the room to the sound of knitting needles furiously clicking as Paul contemplated what I'd told him. As I walked back to my room, I had to laugh at myself. A few months ago, with my heart set on the single scull, I would have bet a million dollars that I would never again row with Paul. Even a few days ago, with my heart set on rowing with Tiff, I would have made the same bet. Once again, time and circumstance had changed, and now I was practically proposing marriage to Paul. Okay - I could do worse.

To celebrate Harry's long feared return to Hanover, Tiff and I drove into town for a beer at the Bulls Eye Bar. Like the Hell Hole Video Parlor, the Bulls Eye was frequented by local, non-Dartmouth people, and I always felt comfortable in the snug of the window booth where I could keep a look-out for stray coaches. The bar's specialty was long neck Rolling Rock beer for $1.15 a bottle, a delicacy not known on the West coast.

As we drank, Tiff and I discussed our options: quit or stay. Tiff was still optimistic about making the quad, but I felt we should abandon Harry's camp. Paul and I were not married, yet.

"We should leave right now," I told him. "We can get a good boat and try our luck at the trials."

"And miss an all-expense-paid trip to Lucerne?" Tiff asked.

"Tiff, you've been to Lucerne. I'm talking about the big trip - to Los Angeles. We might meet Hunter S. Thompson. He'll probably be writing for *Rolling Stone*."

But Tiff wanted no part of my mutiny. For over ten years, he had rowed for Harry, through college, and then on five national teams, and now he was determined to stay by Harry's side.

Tiff had the unique honor of being on two Olympic teams, but without ever having competed in the Olympic Games. In 1976, he had been a spare on the sweep team, and in '80 we were all reduced to the role of spare, thanks to the boycott. With Tiff's actuarial career shifting into high gear, the '84 Games would be his last chance to compete in the Olympics.

I understood Tiff's devotion to the camp quad. Charlie and Joe were flying fast, making my proposed solo effort in the double scull appear very difficult. Only the quad was left. Everyone knew Harry was the best coach. He had good equipment, top scullers, money to burn, even a trip to Lucerne. The quad he selected would dominate the trials. Tiff would certainly be in that quad, giving him a dependable path to the Olympic team.

By stepping outside of Harry's domain, Tiff and I would be taking a huge gamble, perhaps giving up our last chance to make the team.

"But look at the big picture," I said. "If we make the team in the quad, we'll probably get hammered at the Games. We can do better - come on Tiff. Take a chance."

No, no chance of taking a chance - at least for Tiff. Making the team was all that mattered.

We drank our Rolling Rocks and talked of years gone by, when we had an abundance of energy and optimism and fantastic confidence. On bad news days like today, I preferred recalling the past to thinking about the future.

13

ON THE HOT SEAT
JUNE 6, 1984

TO SPEED UP THE SELECTION PROCESS, COACH HARRY immediately abandoned his 2000-meter race format in favor of seat racing.

Each workout became a series of two-minute pieces. After three two-minute pieces, the scullers being seat raced - one man from each boat - would be switched. Another three pieces would be rowed. Now for the moment of truth: if Quad-A was faster than Quad-B before the switch, and then Quad-B was faster than Quad-A after the switch, the man who transferred from A to B was the superior sculler.

To keep the seat racing fair, each sculler, regardless of whether they were being seat raced or not, had to pull his hardest on each piece. The best way to ensure that this happened, at least for the first few pieces, was not to tell the scullers who was being seat raced. Also, eight scullers were needed in order to seat race two quads. With Ridgely and Paul now gone, Harry recruited Charlie and Joe to fill out the boats.

In the first practice after Harry's return, Tiff was matched against Jack Frackleton. Much to everyone's amazement, their seat race was extremely close, or in Harry's words, "a non-victory for both scullers."

How could that happen? Jack Frackleton was a nice guy, but I considered him to be only an average sculler. Tiff, however, was a renowned seat racer. His seat racing prowess was recorded on the huge black and white photo in the stairway of the Harvard Boathouse. Tiff's oar has a tremendous bend, as if he were trying to catapult himself right out of the picture. The contorted, agonized look on his face was pure seat racing beauty.

In the second practice, we again raced three pieces, and then we rested. Within a few seconds, a steaming wave of uncertainty crawled up my neck as Coach Harry's launch slowly motored toward my boat. While growing up I played a few different sports, basketball in high school, volleyball in college, but no aspect of these sports compared with the drama that was now unfolding. The coaching launch, 15 feet away, was drawing inexorably toward one victim. It wheeled around the stern of the quad and angled straight toward the two seat. Then the engine was cut, and in complete silence, it drifted toward the seat racer.

This afternoon, I was that man toward whom the launch drifted, and instantly I asked myself, "Why hadn't I tried harder on that last piece?" I had tried hard, but I was still upright, conscious, which meant some energy, perhaps too much, had been kept in reserve. Too late to worry. The results were already documented history, written on a notepad and buried deep in Harry's duffle bag.

I climbed into Harry's launch, and we lazily motored to the other quad, coming to rest at Sean Colgan's rigger.

Another strange moment occurred as Sean and I exchanged places in the coaching launch. As Sean and I passed, I said, "Good job, keep it up." He looked away and said nothing, as was the usual demeanor of an oarsman in the midst of a seat race. The next few minutes would have a significant impact on both our lives.

Lowering myself in the vacant seat, I looked at my new teammates. Their boat had been doing well, and no doubt the scullers had formed an allegiance, which included the departed Sean Colgan. The allegiance had been severed by an interloper. Sorry, guys. Harry put me here.

A quad moves fastest, not only by the strength and endurance of the four scullers, but by the delicate rhythm they share. When entering a new boat, a champion seat racer like Tiff might say a few words to his boatmates, a positive, sincere line or two, "Good rowing, guys. Now let's uncork a really fast one." By the start of the next piece, Tiff would have already formed a new set of bonds.

I was not a talented seat racer. I couldn't say the right words, and more importantly, I had difficulty funneling all my strength and energy into a short, hyper-intense piece. When fresh and rested, my ability to hammer through a seat race was adequate, occasionally quite good, but now I was tired, distracted, bored, discouraged. I would be lucky to defeat Sean Colgan.

The margin on the next three pieces was close, Coach Harry told us afterwards, but slightly in favor of my opponent. Congratulations to Sean Colgan.

Chris Allsopp was in a talkative mood on the way back to the Chieftain Motel from Goose Pond. As we bounced along the unpaved road, I summoned the courage to ask for an honest evaluation of my standing at camp.

"You haven't been trying," he said. "It's obvious you've been cruising along, feeling sorry for yourself for having lost the single trials."

It wasn't true. Allsopp was wrong. Or maybe he was right. Somewhere during this hated camp, I had fumbled away my sense of self. I could not honestly tell how hard I had been trying. Was Allsopp right? Even slightly crippled, I should have been able to handle these guys - or maybe not. Doubts in the system. Allsopp was wrong, of course he was, and yet he spoke with such authority that I didn't know what to say except, "Go on."

"You lost this morning's seat race," he said, "and now you have only one more chance. If you defeat Bill Purdy tomorrow morning, then you'll be in the quad at the three seat. If you lose, you'll be in the second double, with either Tiff or Jack."

"But what about the stroke seat?" I asked. "Harry hasn't seat raced for the stroke seat."

"Harry has decided on a stroke - Charlie Bracken." Our conversation ended with this bit of bewildering news.

Bracken had not been seat raced, apparently because Coach Harry already knew that Bracken was a fighter, capable of leading his crew to fantastic accomplishments, drawing phenomenal strength from the blast furnace of power that brewed within his soul. I wondered why, if he was such a tremendous fighter, he had not fought his way into semi-finals at the single trials.

As Chris and I turned onto the main highway and headed the last few miles toward the motel, I reflected on the steep, downward path that I had been following this summer. A few weeks ago I had been the second best sculler in the country.

Now I was trying like crazy to avoid being the lowest entity on our eight-man team.

Perhaps the barriers I had erected at the single trials - excluding myself from the sculling fraternity - had caused my failure at the camp. Certainly I could use an ally or two in tomorrow's practice, a couple of guys who especially wanted to see me win the camp's final seat race.

In retrospect, after the single trials I should have had ten days of easy rowing, no racing, to rest up and to relearn the techniques for moving a team boat down the river. But Harry was in charge, and he was in a hurry. We had no time for such esoteric endeavors.

Toward the end of this marathon camp, I found myself anticipating failure in the workouts, and in a strange, self-defeating way, I began to enjoy the pain of my regular losses. Then the sweetness of my long naps, three and fours hours a day, soothed my depression. Once I stayed in bed all day, going in and out of sleep like an opium addict. I kept saying to myself, "just a few more minutes," until the whole day eventually passed without my having escaped the bed.

As I reached the darkest, deepest part of the camp, my naps and nighttime sleep were always preceded by the vivid image of me putting a large-caliber revolver to my right temple and pulling the trigger, instantly painting the curtains of my room a bloody red. During my waking hours, I only thought of backpacking in my beloved Sierra Nevada Mountains. The Sierras loomed as inviting in my waking hours as the revolver in the penumbra of my sleep.

Brad Alan Lewis

14

ONE LAST SEAT RACE
FRIDAY, JUNE 8, 1984

THANKS TO ALLSOPP, BY THE TIME WE PUSHED OFF FROM THE
shore of Goose Pond, the whole team knew that Bill Purdy
and I would be seat raced for the last spot in the quad. Charlie
Altekruse stroked one quad; behind Charlie sat Joe Bouscaren
(Purdy's best friend and roommate); then came Purdy; and
lastly, Tiff in the bow. Ouch. They looked good, very
businesslike, as they paddled away from the shore.

My quad, until Purdy and I switched, was stroked by
Charlie Bracken, then Sean Colgan, myself, and Jack
Frackleton. We pushed away from the shore, swatting
mosquitoes and cursing Goose Pond.

Everyone was thoroughly tired of living at the Chieftain
Motel, not to mention tired of each other, dorm food, Harry,
Chris, and especially Goose Pond. These camps always started
with great expectations, with lots of camaraderie and good
spirit, (although this particular camp seemed to lack those
features from the beginning), but they inevitably drifted into
a tedious, miserable, endless grind. Even our occasional days
off had been tiring.

In a mirror image of our first day in Hanover, a dreary rain settled on our shoulders as we paddled away from the shore. Wait a second. Hold water. Stop the boat. Something felt terribly wrong in the first few strokes. The rhythm was off, our timing was bad, the recovery was tense. Bracken's style, which I had never experienced until this workout, was thoroughly contrary to my own. I had exactly 17 minutes of warm-up time to adjust to Bracken's rhythm, timing, posture, power application, and recovery ratio. On my insistence, we tried a few drills, followed by five minutes of steady rowing. Our boat still felt awful.

"Listen guys," I said, "if things don't improve right away, we're going to get our collective asses handed to us." Usually, I would have said nothing and simply endured the workout. But with my rowing life quickly drawing to a close, I had to make some attempt to alter our downward course. Neither Bracken nor Colgan nor Frackleton said a word in answer to my plea.

Even though we were rowing like beginners, I still maintained a small hope that I could defeat Bill Purdy. I had crushed him in the single scull only a few weeks before. Could the quad be so much different? This final workout - four times three minutes, with Purdy and me being switched after the second piece - would answer all questions.

"Ready?" Harry said, as the boats paddled in sync. "On the next stroke." As the first race began, I remember thinking, "Thankfully this camp is almost over," instead of something inspiring such as, "Let's go after them."

We stayed dead even with Altekruse's boat for about a minute, and then we slowed down. Our quad lacked any pretense of rhythm or swing, and instead we punched at the water as if we were drunk and angry at the same time. Bad,

bad strokes. When our strength wore thin, as I knew it inevitably would, we started to fall behind - first one length, then two - until the other boat appeared like a shadow over my right shoulder. Finally, mercifully, Harry yelled, "Paddle."

I saw him conferring with Allsopp as we took our rest, perhaps verifying that the margin had been as great as it appeared.

Our second piece was no better than the first. Bracken's technique was so contrary, so different from my own that I wondered if he weren't playing a trick on me. I anxiously awaited my departure from Bracken and company.

As Allsopp steered Harry's launch toward me, I summed up my challenge: Purdy's margin of victory averaged six lengths. In order to win the seat race, my new boat, Altekruse's boat, had to win the next two pieces by more than six lengths. Good luck, Lewis.

I felt cold and slightly sick to my stomach as I took my place in Harry's launch. A few inches from me, Harry sat immobile, alone in the bow. As we glided toward the other quad, I said to Harry in my lowest voice, "If you would rather call off the rest of the practice, that would be fine with me."

I was ready to accept the end of my rowing life, but Harry was not. He responded by shifting his gaze from the bottom of the boat to some distant point on the horizon. He wanted this story played to the end. Yes, Harry was right. I had been wrong to suggest the easy solution. Let's play out this madness to the end.

In a few seconds, we arrived at Altekruse's quad, and as Purdy eased himself into the launch, I said to him, "Nice rowing, Bill." To my surprise, I really meant it. Purdy nodded at me, and said, "Thanks," in a very confident voice. Certainly Purdy would fall victim to the same terrible Bracken-technique that I had endured. My new boat might not defeat Bracken's boat by more than the six lengths, but I expected to at least win each piece.

I was wrong. To my everlasting embarrassment, Bracken's boat - with Purdy in my former place - won both pieces by three lengths. Purdy's superiority over me was the first, indisputable, clear-cut conclusion to emerge from the '84 Olympic sculling camp.

For some reason, perhaps because the margin was so decisive, I didn't feel sad or angry or even disappointed. Actually, I felt elated. The camp was over, and I would never have to visit Goose Pond again. For the first time in weeks, I was cheerful and talkative. I helped load the boats onto the trailer with newfound enthusiasm.

An hour later, we returned to the Dartmouth Boathouse for our final team meeting. We stood in a semi-circle, eight tired warriors. Coach Harry Parker stood in front of us with Allsopp to his left.

"The boatings are as follows," Harry said. My stomach muscles tensed, and I felt a sudden urge to run to the toilet. A big part of me was still furious that I had failed so miserably.

"The double will be Charlie and Joe." We knew this already, but Harry reminded us, just in case we had forgotten. "The quad will be Bracken, Purdy, Colgan, and Tiff." They looked down at their feet and smiled. Their moment of victory had arrived. Olympic bound lads. Their parents would scream with delight when they heard the news.

If I had felt the urge to cry, the misty rain would have provided the perfect cover. No crying for me. My only urge was to be far away from Harry and Hanover.

"Brad and Jack will row the double in Lucerne on Saturday," Harry continued. "On Sunday, I want to give Jack a try in the quad, so Tiff and Brad will race the double. I'll see you guys at the Harvard Boathouse tomorrow morning at 6:30 for an easy practice."

The results were now official. I was the lowest entity on our eight-man squad, and I immediately invented a new title to describe my station: spare's spare.

Either Jack or Tiff was the true spare. One of them would eventually be awarded the ignominious role of Olympic spare.

By my calculation, an even lower place was reserved for me. I was the spare's spare, the ultimate odd man out - the extra, extra man. I would amuse Tiff or Jack until it was his turn to row in the quad.

In the first few minutes that followed Harry's speech, I felt all manner of nasty emotions welling up inside me, "You don't know shit about rowing and even less about people." The least hostile of those emotions was a desire to have a Rolling Rock at 10:15 A.M..

Suddenly Charlie asked, "What about the rowing clothes we're supposed to get?"

Everyone laughed, a bit uneasily, wondering if Harry's unpredictable sense of humor was suitably warmed up for Charlie's flippant question.

"I'll find out about the clothes this afternoon," Harry said, in a calm, slightly amused voice. "And I'll give you the details of the trip after the morning practice. I know the plane for Zurich leaves around six o'clock tomorrow evening."

One last time I rode with Chris Allsopp to the Chieftain Motel.

"So, things didn't go my way this morning," I said.

Chris laughed at my understatement. "You're lucky to be going on the trip."

"Yeah, well, that's true. In fact, I'm considering not going to Lucerne."

The line came out of my mouth before I'd even had a chance to consider what I was saying, as though for once the barrier between my feelings and my words had disappeared.

Chris looked surprised. No one in the history of U.S. rowing had ever declined an all-expense paid trip to Europe.

"I'd advise you to make the trip to Lucerne," he said. "After all, what have you got to lose?"

"Paul Enquist, for one thing," I said. "If I stay home, I can hook up with Paul, and we can practice before the double trials."

Chris contemplated this idea for a few seconds and then said, "You'll still have plenty of time to practice with Paul after you come back from Europe. If you quit now, all your other options are lost."

"I have no other options."

"How about you and Jack in a double, or you and Tiff?" Chris asked. "In Lucerne, you'll get a chance to race with both of them."

"Jack is a nice guy, but there's no way in hell I'll race the trials with him. I'd love to row with Tiff. I told you that when the camp started."

"Yeah, well, Harry knew you wanted to row with him because I told him. He had other ideas, obviously."

"It's too late now," I said. "I'm sure Harry will put Tiff in the quad. Besides, the only practice Tiff and I would get in Lucerne would be rowing from the dock to the starting line on Sunday. How could anyone call that a true test of our ability?"

"Think it over carefully," Chris said. "You'll be making a big mistake if you quit the team. If things go poorly in Lucerne, then quit after you get home. What do you think Paul is going to do - row with Ridgely?"

I had to laugh at the image of these two giants rowing together. In one practice, Paul and Ridgely had raced the double, finishing lengths behind the winner. Usually, bigger is better in rowing - more muscle, a longer reach, a bigger lever with which to pry the boat across the water. But Paul and Ridgely were too big. They had twice the driving power of a smaller crew, but they lacked the finesse to keep the speed from falling away on the recovery.

As I packed my gear, Harry stuck his head through the open door. "Let me know your decision by 5:00 this afternoon," he said abruptly.

I felt embarrassed by Harry's unexpected appearance and angry with Allsopp for having such a big fucking mouth.

"Right," I said, accidentally borrowing Harry's unique clipped pronunciation of the word. He glanced at me a second time, wondering if I was mocking him. He left my room, muttering some words I didn't catch, and shaking his head.

Harry had used over five weeks to make his decisions, and now I had five hours and forty-five minutes to make mine. Not a minute to waste.

15

"BIG NOTHING" VERSUS "BIG GAMBLE"
12:01 P.M., FRIDAY, JUNE 8, CONTINUED

WITH MY BAGS PACKED, I BEGAN SEARCHING FOR A QUIET RIDE to Boston. I needed privacy during the three-hour drive, time to think, time to decide my future. Not surprisingly, with my sunken status I had a difficult time securing a ride. Finally, Joe Bouscaren, the passenger seat of his VW Rabbit obviously vacant, reluctantly granted my request.

"Sure, why not," he said, as if I were a scruffy hitchhiker caught in a rainstorm. "Climb in."

"Great. Thanks Joe."

"Oh, and by the way," Joe said, "my friend Sarah is going to ride with us to Boston."

"That's fine with me," I said, "I'm just going to keep to myself."

With Joe at the wheel, and Sarah chatting next to him, I tried to make up my mind: Quit or stay. *Quit* is a terrible word, and the mere prospect of being termed a *quitter* almost convinced me to stay with the squad. What would Carl Hilterbrand do in my place? He'd probably cut off Harry's nose with a Skilsaw.

At the conclusion of this morning's team meeting, Harry had extended his hand to me, not to shake hands, but to give me a $20 bill. As of today I was on the Olympic dole. From now until the Closing Ceremonies, I would not be required to pry apart my wallet and use my own money, except to pay for beer and video games. This $20 installment was supposed to buy our meals until we left for Lucerne. Had I entered into a tacit agreement to stay with Harry by accepting the money? I could always give it back, I suppose. I didn't know what to do: quit or stay.

My notebook became my only confidant on the drive to Boston, and within its pages I debated the possible outcomes from each path. A hundred obstacles loomed ahead if I quit. I'd need a boat, a car for transporting it, not to mention a partner. Where would we train? I scribbled four pages of notes, made even more indecipherable by the endless bouncing of the little car. Those pages will forever remain my favorite piece of writing.

On the third page of my notes, I outlined the probable itinerary for the Lucerne trip. Between the four travel days, two race days, and two recovery days, I concluded that relative to my own selfish interests, the Lucerne trip was a jumbled mess. Travel days were more tiring than shopping at South Coast Plaza the day before Christmas. Race and recovery days, although great fun, wouldn't advance my goal of winning the Olympic trials. If I went to Lucerne, I would return to the U.S. in poor physical shape - even worse than now. And after the trip, only eight days would remain until the trials. Eight puny days. Hmm. Eight days was not enough time to make much improvement in boat speed. You might be able to get sick in eight days, but you couldn't get well.

Staying home, with the right partner, looked far more

productive. That right partner was Paul. No other sculler in the U.S. could handle the regimen I had in mind, except perhaps Tiff, and he was long gone. It had to be Paul.

First, we would take a few days rest, just easy rowing, maybe some technique stuff, and then we'd go into a hard-training phase. Lots of 500-meter pieces - yes, lots and lots of 500s. Then we'd get good and rested. Finally, the double trials. Altogether, we'd have a 21-day, uninterrupted run to the trials. We could build a castle in 21 days - as long as we quickly solved the equipment problems.

One question kept popping into my head as the drive progressed: was Paul committed to another partner? I hadn't seen or heard from him in a few days. Maybe he was already chopping bait on the poop deck of his Dad's fishing boat.

At the bottom of the first page, on the right-hand side, was the key to my life: 'Might go w/ Paul.'

Yes, it might go, might go fast, might go wonderfully fast with Paul. We were good last year. Maybe we could go even faster. Only one way to find out. My grand goal was to make the Olympic team - as a participant. Even if Harry offered me the spare spot, I could not accept it. Some people knew how to handle that role, but not me. My soul demanded action. I lived to participate, not to watch.

As the long drive concluded, I wrote this line: 'Lucerne, big nothing. Staying home, big gamble.' Okay, enough writing. In some form or another, I had thought these thoughts ten thousand times during the course of the camp. Yes, these thoughts were old, but the potential for action was brand new.

I made my decision: Adios, Harry. Later, guys. Fresh start. New partner. New life. I'll pay the bills. No time to search the annals of rowing history for a precedent. I had tolerated my self-imposed prison long enough. Time to break free.

From this moment I would live by my hard work and by my cleverness, both driven by a deep undercurrent of anger. This anger came from my failure at the camp, from the smug attitude of Charlie and his friends, from losing the single trials. With Harry as my master, I had been drowning in this anger. Now I could let it flow. If properly directed, anger is the best, most powerful motivator.

The responsibility for success or failure would be all mine, like in the bad old days. I was ready. No, I was overly ready, by about five weeks.

As soon as we arrived at the Harvard Boathouse, I unfolded my legs from the back seat and ran to the phone to call my Dad for a quick confirmation.

"There's no way you can make the Olympic team if you go to Lucerne," my Dad agreed. "If you row with Jack, you'll lose to Charlie and Joe at the trials. And Tiff will probably be in the quad. Right?"

"Yeah," I said. "But maybe Harry will put me in the quad if they do lousy in Lucerne."

"But you don't want to be in the quad."

"No way," I said. "Quads are a drag."

"Then grab Paul and get going," he said. "The sooner you split from Harry, the better off you'll be."

Grabbing Paul turned out to be the easiest task of all. After talking to my Dad, I went back to Joe's Rabbit to retrieve my bags. Joe and Sarah had departed, but they had thoughtfully left my gear in the parking lot. As I placed my bags on the boathouse porch, I saw Paul walking toward me.

Time for action. No more smokescreens, delays, hassles. When he arrived, I said: "I want to row the double with you. Do you want to go for it?"

"Yes, okay," Paul said, with a huge smile. "Count me in."

We shook hands and sealed our partnership. Married on Friday, June 8, 1984. Every good adventure started on a Friday, or maybe I had that wrong. Old time mariners refused to start a journey on a Friday because that was the day Christ was crucified. Superstitious? You better believe it. I was in a hurry, too. I firmly believe all good adventures begin on whatever day they happen to start.

One tiny distasteful chore still remained to be completed. At 4:55 P.M. I called Harry to let him know my decision. Harry answered, and for a few seconds I fumbled for the right words, the quitting words. Paul was standing a few feet away, making faces, trying to offer advice on what to say.

Finally I said, "Harry, I've decided to come to Lucerne after all." Paul jerked to attention, wondering if I had changed my mind.

"Great," said Harry.

"But only," I continued, "if Paul and I can row the double together."

A long pause followed, long enough for Paul to walk over and slap me on the back in recognition of my killing joke. I pictured Harry scanning the shotguns on the wall in his den, trying to decide which one to use to blow my head off.

"Well," Harry said, regaining himself, "that wouldn't be fair to Jack, now, would it?"

I laughed involuntarily. Fairness seemed a remote concern at this stage. "Jack's a great guy and all," I said, "but it has to be me and Paul, or I don't make the trip."

"I see. Well, in that case I guess you don't make the trip."

Harry said a few other things designed to make me feel bad about abandoning the squad. Finally I said, "Sorry it didn't work out as planned, but you're going to have to find yourself another boy." Then I hung up.

As I walked out of the boathouse, I saw my campmates, or more accurately, my former campmates, in the parking lot unloading the boat trailer. I watched them for a few seconds while I considered the next course of action. My first desire was to leave Boston, or at least the boathouse, before Harry appeared with 12-gauge in hand.

Paul came through with a good suggestion, his first of many: "How about if we go to Squam Lake with Curtis and his guys? I was planning to go with them before you showed up."

"What the heck is Squam Lake?" I asked.

Someone came out of the boathouse right then and shouted, "Paul, you've got a phone call. It's Harry." Paul and I looked at each other, and without a word he walked inside.

A minute later, Paul returned and said, "Harry offered me a spot on the team."

"What'd you tell him?"

"I said I'd think about it." What had I gotten myself into? Our marriage wasn't ten minutes old, and already Paul wanted an annulment.

"So call him back," I said, "and tell him to get screwed."

While Paul declined Harry's offer, I walked toward Curtis Fleming's truck to have a few words with my old high school crewmate. Curtis was loading a quad onto the roof of his truck in preparation for a private rowing weekend at Squam Lake, located deep in the heart of New Hampshire.

"Would you mind if I tagged along with you?" I asked.

"Sure," Curtis said. "Come along, we have plenty of room."

"Do you have room for a boat on your roof, too?"

"Yeah, throw it on, but make it fast 'cause we're leaving in five minutes."

We needed a boat. A few doubles from the Hanover camp still remained on the trailer, and I set my sights on a tattered Carbocraft double scull, the oldest, although not the worst boat to survive the camp.

Without a word, I walked to the trailer and began untying the Carbocraft. When Paul reemerged a minute later, we lifted the Carbocraft off the trailer, and, instead of walking into the boathouse - the proper destination - we jogged to Curtis's truck, and quickly secured it to the roof rack. We were not stealing the boat, we were borrowing it, with permission to be requested at a later date.

Then we sifted through the jumbled mess of oars lying next to the trailer.

"Which oars do you want to take?" Paul asked.

"I want the two sets we used last year," I said. "The ones marked 'G' and 'H.' You know, for Go to Hell."

I expected Harry to drive up at any moment and spoil our act of liberation, but only Charlie Altekruse interrupted the fun.

"Where you going with our boat and oars?" Charlie asked.

"They're mine now," I said.

"That's just like you, Lewis," Charlie said. "If things aren't going your way, you quit."

"What's wrong, Charlie?" I said. "Is your sure spot on the Olympic Team not quite so sure anymore?"

If I had ever considered a friendship with Charlie, the next few words we exchanged, mostly obscene, would forever prevent that possibility.

Before the storm could break, Paul and I were on our way to Squam Lake.

The rafters shook and jammed the next morning at the Harvard Boathouse. A friend of mine, who happened to be in the boathouse at that time, told me later that Harry was madder than anyone had ever seen him. He called a special team meeting where he screamed about the need for loyalty and team unity.

"Just one thoughtless, self-centered guy LIKE LEWIS can screw it up for everyone," Harry screamed.

The remaining seven scullers looked at each other and nodded in agreement. I wonder if any of them were thinking they might like to be in my shoes, taking control of their fate as opposed to trusting Harry. Maybe one or two, the Philly guys perhaps. Watching Coach Harry screaming in front of them would have quickly banished those thoughts. Harry was a frightening man when he was angry - I'd seen him in action, up close, right in my face. No doubt their fear of Harry was greater than their fear of fate.

I considered my actions to be correct, necessary, essential to the nurturing of my soul - my brand new soul. Point of view is all important. Harry had a different point of view. So be it. We'd settle our differences at the Olympic double scull trials.

16

ROCKYWOLD HONEYMOONERS, PAUL AND BRAD
5:15 P.M., FRIDAY, JUNE 8, CONTINUED

AS WE DROVE AWAY FROM THE HARVARD BOATHOUSE, MY
world changed from a tired black and white movie to a
brilliant, living color, 3-D epic. I'd never felt happier in my
life. To be free from Harry and the camp was pure heaven.

I rode in a vintage Fury III, driven by Mike Totta, a sculler
who had not been invited to Harry's camp. Totta's Fury III
reminded me of my old Mercury Montego, waiting for me in
southern California. My Montego's battery was certainly dead
after so many dormant months. It would need recharging,
much like my soul needed recharging - or more accurately,
replacing.

Our destination was Squam Lake, the site of *On Golden
Pond*, in the middle of New Hampshire, and for the first 80
miles, we traversed the same road that I had traveled only an
hour before. By now the repetitive freeway foliage was beginning to resemble the background of a kid's cartoon, and
although I wanted to sleep, I had too much adrenalin
coursing through my veins to even close my eyes.

As the miles rolled along, I took stock of my new mates who had so abruptly replaced the last team. Ridgely Johnson shared the back seat with Paul and myself. His enormous size, 6'8" and 235 pounds, directly contradicted his restrained, Ivy League demeanor. Ridgely slept for most of the drive. Mike Totta, nicknamed Tots, drove the car. He had taken a year's leave from medical school to pursue his Olympic sculling dream. Gregg Montesi sat next to Totta. Gregg, a recent graduate of the Naval Academy, had been a champion youth sculler. He sculled beautifully and was quiet and exceptionally polite - a rare combination among American scullers. I vaguely remembered Gregg from the junior varsity group at Harry's camp.

Through the windshield I saw Curtis Fleming's truck leading the way, laden with boats and oars. Curtis's new wife, Nancy, shared the cab, along with Bruce Beall, formerly of Harry's camp, and his fiancée, Barb Trafton. Curtis and I had rowed a double together in '82 - a big slow mistake on my part. We both lived in Newport Beach, although we didn't train side by side nearly enough for my taste. Despite our having rowed together in high school and a little in college, Curtis was not a big fan of mine. I wasn't sure of the reason although it might have had something to do with the inordinate pleasure I derived from waking him down from one end of Newport Harbor to the other.

My nickname for Curtis was 7-Up, as in "Never had it, never will." He called me, when I wasn't around, *Brad Clueless*. These childish games were no longer appropriate, as if they ever had been, and I made a particular effort to be on my best behavior with everyone.

The first task of Curtis and his four mates was to eliminate one man and then proceed with a few weeks of training.

At the Olympic quad trials, also being held in Princeton at the same time as the double trials, they hoped to catch Harry's quad on an exceptionally bad day.

I figured Curtis's quad had only a slim chance of winning the trials. Individually, they had some varying abilities. Bruce and Gregg rowed with excellent technique. Ridgely had fantastic strength, and Totta was a steady performer. All five men had raced internationally, which was extremely important at the high-pressure Olympic trials. Curtis's team had one other thing going in their favor. Secretly for some, openly for others, the team members felt that Harry had wrongly ignored them, and now they hungered for a chance to prove their ability.

Four hours later we arrived at Squam Lake, or more specifically, a family-run campground on the lake's north shore, Rockywold-Deephaven Camp. Bruce Beall had suggested this perfect weekend retreat, with its miles and miles of smooth, open water. I soon became a big fan of Squam Lake, so wonderfully removed from the tumultuous Charles River.

The owner's hospitality and the excellent bass fishing attracted Rockywold's devoted patrons, and each summer the same families stayed in the same cabins. The cabins had ice boxes, kept cool with ice that had been cut from the lake the previous winter. The owner told me that he had replaced these antiques with refrigerators a few years back, but the guests preferred the quaintness of the old-fashioned ice boxes. With great pride, he claimed to be the only innkeeper to have converted from refrigerators to ice boxes.

By financial necessity, our stay would not be long. Although the price included excellent waffles, fresh fruit, and homemade ice cream, Rockywold was not cheap by rower standards, $40 a day. Perhaps I should have paid an entertainment surcharge because my room was sandwiched between our two amorous couples.

Paul and I saved our energy for rowing. Over the next two days, we spent a total of 13 hours on the water - six workouts - practicing easy technical drills. Catch only, two inches of slide only, arms and back only, arms only, eyes closed. Sometimes we rowed with only one oar at a time, so that we scribed huge circles on the surface of the lake.

In a sense, we were worse than beginners. Our technique had been thoroughly altered in Hanover, and not for the better. We needed a few days of easy rowing, no pressure, slow technical sculling, before advancing to more difficult tasks.

Rowing is an absurdly simple sport. I can easily guide a beginner through the right technical motions. The difficulty arises when that beginner attempts to repeat those motions on a bumpy racecourse, at 40 strokes a minutes, with his heart rate zooming and an opponent charging up his stern. Paul and I inevitably returned to the basics. Nothing else existed.

Somewhere along the way, preferably sooner than later, double scull partners must blend together. Egos must be deflated and cast aside. Any problems must be smoothed out and some basic harmony established. Sculling teams comprising two brothers, Frank and Alf Hansen for example, have a huge advantage. They can scream and curse at each other when things go bad, as always happened for at least a few practices each month, without worrying that their partnership will be permanently damaged. Brothers will always be brothers.

A honeymoon such as Paul and I were enjoying had rarely been seen in the great northeast. Two big brutes, stuffed into a tiny boat, plying the distant back channels of Squam Lake -

we simply wanted to be alone. With heads bent close, we talked at breakfast and dinner, plotting how we would overcome our opponents. Paul and I were very different people, and not necessarily drawn toward a bond of friendship. But with our handshake, now two days old, I reshuffled my feelings toward him. He was no longer the awkward fisherman from Seattle, a tad clumsy, and more than a tad uncool by southern California standards. As of last Friday, Paul was my savior, a straight-up guy with whom I would eagerly entrust my life. And since when had southern California cool ever won a race? Paul was honest to a fault, a fighter, a survivor, a man with a mission. In his soul, he carefully harbored the all-consuming spark of insane physical expression that would thrust us to victory. Or at least I hoped he did.

Harry desperately needed an eighth sculler to complete his squad, and not surprisingly, he looked to the north, Squam Lake, for the missing man.

During breakfast Saturday morning, Ridgely Johnson was called to the phone. A minute later he returned and announced, "I'm going to Lucerne with Harry's team."

Paul and I kept eating, hardly losing a beat in our consumption of cereal, but for Curtis and his mates, breakfast was suspended. They convened an impromptu team meeting - a minute later, they filed back into the room, all smiles and laughter. Ridgely was calling Allsopp at this very moment to cancel his contract.

An hour later Allsopp, who did all of Coach Harry's bidding, asked Gregg Montesi to report for Olympic sculling squad duty. Once again, request denied.

Thus on Saturday night, Harry's squad flew to Lucerne with only seven scullers. Never in the history of U.S. rowing had an individual rower, much less four rowers, Gregg, Ridgely,

Paul, and myself, turned down an all-expenses-paid trip to Europe.

Also included in the Lucerne trip was a lovely assortment of authentic Olympic rowing clothes: jerseys, socks, warm-up pants, all neatly folded into a team issue travel bag. The bag also contained two pairs of national team rowing shorts, dark blue, with a thin stripe of red and white piping down the sides. These coveted shorts had a special meaning. For decades U.S. oarsmen, myself included, had dreamed of owning these simple, unobtrusive rowing shorts. This one item of clothing acknowledged to the rest of the rowing world that you had earned a place on the elite squad. You had arrived at the top.

Of course, when Harry's squad completed its Lucerne adventure, these clothes would have to be returned to the U.S. rowing federation. Harry's double and quad were not official Olympians, at least not until they went through the formalities of winning the Olympic trials. But in an act of bravado, each member of Harry's squad wrote his name in the borrowed clothes with an indelible laundry pen. They cursed us, hated us, despised our insubordination. The Squam Lake Seven would be demolished at the trials, and the precious rowing clothes would never have to be returned.

Rockywold served us well. We earned a big jump on correcting our technical faults, and now that Harry and his troops had departed, Paul and I could emerge from hiding and pursue our most needed commodity - hard, stinging, relentless competition. Paul and I agreed that our success at the 1983 World Championships was due to the brutal train-ing we had endured against an excellent four-with coxswain.

A four-with coxswain, usually called a 'four-with,' is made up of four sweep oarsmen plus a steersman. A world class double scull can move at almost the same speed as a fast four-with. Actually, a double scull is a shade slower on longer pieces, thus the double must work harder to keep up with a speedy four-with.

Sunday afternoon, after a few phone calls, Paul found the competitive solution to our quest. A sweep camp was about to start in Ithaca, New York, one of the few training sites that neither Paul nor I had encountered in our marathon rowing careers.

"The head coach is Tony Johnson from Yale," Paul said, relaying his phone conversation to me. "He has three four-with's waiting to race us. We're welcome to join them. What should I tell him?"

"Tell him we'll be in Ithaca tomorrow," I said, "in time for the afternoon workout."

Brad Alan Lewis

17

ITHACA
SUNDAY, JUNE 10, 1984

LATE SUNDAY NIGHT, ON THE DESERTED STEPS OF THE HARVARD Boathouse, Paul and I said goodbye to our Squam Lake brothers. For work and housing reasons, and because they had nothing to fear from Harry Parker, Curtis and his team-mates had elected to continue training in Boston until the trials, 18 days away. Over the weekend, Mike Totta had been voted out of their squad. That left Bruce, Ridgely, Gregg, and Curtis to work whatever magic they could in the next few weeks. I wished them luck.

The next morning, standing in front of the counter at the Cambridge Budget Rent-a-Car, I withdrew from my wallet the tool I planned to use as often as necessary to satisfy our obsession - plastic money. VISA, American Express, Mastercard, Shell Card, along with cash advance, savings, and money market account, I pillaged every monetary source at my disposal.

Paul, who worked much harder to earn his money than I, wanted to hitch a ride to Ithaca with some college rowers who were driving to Tony Johnson's sweep camp, but I insisted that we rent a car. Hitching was cheaper, but the possibility for delays and hassles was too great. "To hell with the cost," I told Paul. "We can't be relying on anyone."

By summer's end, I had eventually handed over every dollar I owned, and a few thousand I had yet to earn.

Around three in the afternoon, we drove our rented Renault, with our liberated double scull and oars strapped to the roof, across the Ithaca city limits. A half-mile later, we crested a long sweeping hill. To the left sprawled the town of Ithaca. To the right was our destination, Lake Cayuga. In our quest for the ultimate oasis, the lake received all our attention. Every man or woman who has ever rowed, even for only one semester in college, will initially judge all bodies of water - lake, river, ocean, pond, anything bigger than a swimming pool - by its potential to provide a good rowing workout.

I slowed the car to a walking pace and our eyes feasted on the stunning view. The lake rolled to the north, far into the horizon. I marveled at the undeveloped shoreline. Unlike Newport Harbor, where every inch of waterfront was covered with a towering mansion or a fancy restaurant, Lake Cayuga's shoreline was marked by only a few distant houses.

At first, the watery expanse and the pristine shore caught my attention. Then my eyes focused on the ten million white-caps dotting the lake. Gusts of wind were painting dark patches on the surface that evolved into yet another batch of white caps. Wind is the enemy of all rowers. Even small wakes could splash over our boat's three-inch gunnel. If those wakes persisted, our boat would eventually fill with water. From our lofty vantage point, rowing and Lake Cayuga seemed to have little in common.

The wind was blowing directly down the length of the lake, creating two foot tall waves that crashed into a low jetty. White plumes of spray rocketed into the air from the broad-side attack.

"Plenty of rough water practice this afternoon," I said, and we both laughed at my understatement. With luck, a sturdy ship might venture onto the lake without sinking.

Ten minutes later we parked in front of the Cornell Boat-house, a grey, cinder block building with a few strands of ivy clinging to the outer walls. Paul and I walked to the edge of the cement ramp and then onto one of the four wooden docks. To my great surprise only small waves lapped against the dock, rather than the huge rollers we had seen from the hill.

Despite the winds, the sheltering jetty made the water perfectly adequate for rowing. Seeing this barely ruffled water was a great moment. Our seven-hour drive from Boston had not been wasted. Paul and I suited up, had our boat off the roof, rigged, and on the water in less than 15 minutes.

On our maiden voyage, we explored a maze of channels, the largest inland marina in New York, a proud local sailor told me. We tested the waterways like curious dogs. After a few dead-ends and wrong turns, we found our home - a storm channel, used to control the spring runoff, and far removed from the rough and tumble lake. The storm channel was slightly under 1500 meters long and barely wide enough for three boats across, straight and true. At the end of the channel, a full mile from the lake, the water was dead still, glimmering like glass.

"Paul, this is it," I said. "No tide or wind to screw up our times. This is the best 500 meter course I've ever seen. And we'll always have a stretch of good water for practicing technique."

The problem with rowing is time - not time to practice but accurate measurements of time over some portion of the racecourse, from 500 to 2000 meters. Strong tides, as in Newport Beach, howling wind, a problem anywhere, and non-stop current, notorious on Philadelphia's Schuylkill River, are the three destroyers of accurate rowing times. Our new home, this private storm channel on the outskirts of Ithaca, New York, was almost totally unaffected by these variables.

When we returned to the boathouse from our sightseeing tour, we were greeted with stares and hushed whisperings from Tony Johnson's boys.

"Yeah, that's them."

"Those are the guys that blew off Harry."

"They don't look very big to me."

"Which one's Lewis?"

I was surprised and a little flattered to hear that word of our on-going adventure had preceded us. The camp's two coaches, Tony Johnson and Fin Meislahn, stood nearby, looking amused. I assumed, in my newcomer paranoia, that they were laughing at us, but I was wrong. They were laughing at Fin's perennially wet Golden Retriever, Charlie, who was hiding in a tiny crawl space between the ramp and the dock.

"So, you made it," Tony said, sticking out his hand. "I'm glad you're here."

Tony was tall and slim, dressed in faded jeans and a flannel shirt. Over his shirt he wore a strokewatch, the common medallion of rowing coaches around the world. Tony looked exactly like the pictures I had seen of him, except his hair was now completely grey. A promotional poster made by the U.S. rowing federation showed a picture of Tony and his partner, Larry Hough, winning their Olympic silver medal at the 1968 Mexico City Games. This poster adorned almost every boathouse in the country. I could have recognized Tony's lean silhouette a mile away.

Tony's welcoming words sounded honest and straightforward, two qualities that I greatly welcomed. Rowers and coaches in the U.S. are strange, territorial, unpredictable beasts.

Tony Johnson was an exception. I eventually learned that he did not allow jealousy, grudges, or gossip into his being. I really liked Tony.

Fin Meislahn stood next to Tony. He, too, had a similar, free world outlook on rowing. During the school year, Fin coached Cornell's crew. This summer he had volunteered his boathouse and his services to assist Tony. Fin was dressed in more casual coaching attire, khaki shorts and a Blackie's Bar T-shirt, tattered deck shoes, and no socks. On his left ankle he sported a thick, mold-green tattoo of an anchor, a souvenir from his years in the Navy. Both Tony and Fin gave every appearance of being a pair of cool, independent coaches, and in this instance, appearances held form.

"You're welcome to stay in the boathouse," Fin said.

Fin's hospitality caught me off guard, and I had to think a moment before replying. Fin knew nothing about us except that we had run afoul of Coach Harry, although perhaps that alone defined us as oarsmen in need.

Brad Alan Lewis

18

THE SKELETON CREW
MONDAY, JUNE 11, 1984

THE NEXT MORNING WE STOOD ON THE SAME DOCK, INTENTLY listening to Tony's workout instructions: "Head out to the lake," he said. "Row a hundred hard strokes for your warm-up, and be ready to go in 20 minutes. We'll meet in front of the big smokestack."

"What's the workout?" I asked.

"I can't tell you yet," Tony said, "and besides, you don't want to know." Tony always kept his workout plans a secret until the last minute.

Following Tony's orders, we paddled through the break-water to the open expanse of Lake Cayuga. The lake was flat and calm, a remarkable contrast to the previous afternoon. We wouldn't need the storm channel this morning, not with 35 miles of impeccable water straight ahead.

An oarsman needs water to row. Imitating the sport on a rowing machine, although a great winter diversion in the frozen northeast, is not the way to become a champion sculler. For our special mission, Paul and I needed ten billion gallons spread over ten thousand acres.

For one instant I closed my eyes and thanked Tony, thanked luck, thanked Paul, thanked the whole damned universe. Finally, I was surrounded by the ingredients I needed: a good partner, a decent boat, the right coaches, tough competition, and a solitary expanse of water. The most important ingredient - the X factor, the spark, the catalyst, the trigger - was the fire within me, hotter and brighter than the sun. My new soul.

At the conclusion of the single trials, my former soul had dislodged itself and fallen away, destined to become a permanent fixture on the muddy bottom of Lake Carnegie. At Harry's camp, that void had been filled with self-doubt, pity, and other destructive forms of wadding. Now I had to train my new soul to plumb the depths of physical expression, all the way to Hell and back, and not an inch less.

'A hungry dog hunts best,' is an old saying. My new soul was ravenous. Okay, I was ready. Let the fun begin.

Between warm-up pieces, I looked at our competition: three four-with's glided over the unbroken water. These oarsmen, mostly college rowers, had joined Tony's camp to prepare for the Olympic four-with coxswain trials. Like ourselves, they had only the slightest chance of winning.

Another boat, a straight-four, four sweep oarsmen without a coxswain, raced through our flotilla. I looked at them as they jetted past, and then I quickly looked again. This boat appeared to be manned by four skeletons. Their cheekbones stood out like knots, their ribs were clearly defined as if they were painted on. Every leg and arm muscle showed as taut as steel cabling. Four pairs of deep-set eyes peered at us, conveying 'the look.' Their message stated simply: "Are you ready to race? Before this workout is over, we're going to kick your heavyweight asses from one end of this lake to the other."

The four men who were rowing that shell were a special breed of oarsmen, known as *lightweights*, with a 155-pound average weight, and a 159-pound maximum, according to FISA rules. They rowed well, and like most lightweights, they looked lean, intense, and just plain ornery. Maybe we could do a little sparring with them, I thought, as we bounced in their wake. I found out later that a world class lightweight straight-four was exactly the same speed as double scull of similar ability.

Separate lightweight events are held at the World Rowing Championships but not at the Olympic Games. Thus, when competing at the Olympics, lightweights are required to race against heavyweights, or *fatweights*, as they called us. Because of this perceived injustice, lightweights were especially ornery during the Olympic year.

"Who are those guys?" I asked Paul.

"I don't know," he said, "but they look pretty good."

"Today's workout is four times five minutes at race rate," Tony yelled through his megaphone. "There will be plenty of rest between pieces, so go like hell."

A loud moan went up from the college rowers as they heard Tony's announcement. Harry might have thrown down his megaphone at this insubordination, but Tony only laughed. Our boat was nearest the coaching launch, and I heard him say to Fin, "If they think that's bad, wait until this afternoon's workout."

Paul and I learned a lesson during that workout: 'Double Sculling, 101A,' as taught by the lightweight straight-four. As promised, the lightweights pummeled us from one end of the lake to the other. My neck ached by the end of the workout from craning to confirm the extent of their lead. The lightweights handled us easily on the first piece, and again on the second. On the third piece, we stayed even until the last minute, and then they pulled away, as though shifting into overdrive on the sharp commands of their bowman.

On the last piece, we only saw their wake.

"Those guys are fast," Paul said, as we paddled toward the boathouse after the last piece.

"Yeah, you're right. Let's see if we can't get their number by the trials," I said. "We'll have to improve everything - technique, endurance, consistency. The main thing we have to improve is our intensity. Those lightweights were rowing as though Jaws was snapping at their stern. From now on, we'll do the same."

Like a tiny snowball set free from a mountain top, that first workout started us rolling, slow at first, gaining speed and size every day. Paul and I worked well together. We made a good team. If this had been an ordinary rowing camp, we would have walked away from each other after practice, leaving Coach Harry to solve any problems. But now we stayed close.

At least once a day, we talked with Tony and Fin, who provided us with technical advice. We spent an hour each afternoon watching videos, not of ourselves, but of champion scullers like Norway's Hansen & Thorsen. But mainly Paul and I rowed, hard and long, feasting on the little successes that we encountered within each workout - a decent 500 meter time in the back channel, or staying with the straight-four a few seconds longer on a five-minute piece.

Tony's workouts consisted of standard multiplication tables, 5X5 minutes, 4X3 minutes, 10X2 minutes, 6X3 minutes, all at maximum-effort race pace. I preferred some varying number of five-minute pieces. Five minutes is a good distance - not so short that you could hold your breath for the duration, but not so long that you couldn't do several pieces through the course of a workout. We often rowed 5X5 minutes in the morning, and then three or four more five-minute pieces in the afternoon. By the trials, Paul and I had dozens of five-minute pieces stashed into our bag of tricks.

Best of all, I didn't dread the tough work, as had been the case only a week before at Harry's camp. Instead, I welcomed the challenge, and I relished the inevitable pain. Intense rowing, the kind that really pushed me to the edge, had always given birth to a raw, wild, electric feeling of pure energy. I don't know any name for that emotion, but I truly loved it. That emotion had been missing in Hanover, but in Ithaca it came back with a vengeance.

In our first days in Ithaca, we intimidated a few of Tony's college rowers. They had never seen two such passionate men, willing to do anything, row any distance, feel any pain, in order to meet their goal. The passion, the intensity that Paul and I demonstrated, startled a lot of people through the course of the summer. This startled reaction made me feel as if our work was paying off. Our best asset was our intensity, and we sought to strengthen it every single day.

Brad Alan Lewis

19

NEW 'DO
JUNE 11, 1984

AFTER BREAKFAST, PAUL AND I WENT TO THE LOCAL SHOPPING center, Triphammer Mall. Paul needed to buy shampoo and toothpaste. I had a slightly bigger mission in mind. I wanted to get a haircut. The perfect time had arrived for me to alter my outside appearance and become an extra-ugly brute.

To Paul's dismay, I still sported my goatee, which I had grown only a few weeks earlier in tribute to the Laker's Magic Johnson. Now that the Lakers had lost to the Celtics in the NBA finals, I considered shaving it off, but my goatee was so remarkably unattractive that I decided to keep it.

Outside appearances are important. My inside appearance, how I felt inside, was already well defined and intact. But I had a theory: if I wanted to row like a mean ugly brute, I had to feel like a mean ugly brute. The best way to feel mean and ugly was to look mean and ugly. A Marine-short haircut was the order of the day.

As Gene the Barber attempted to follow my instructions, I read about a Ferrari that went 110 miles an hour in third gear. After ten minutes, Gene said he was finished, but without looking in the mirror I knew he was wrong.

"Not short enough," I said. "Keep clipping."

My instructions had been simple enough. I wanted to look like a Marine on his first day of boot camp. I had to remind Gene three or four times before he believed the sincerity of my message.

When we left Triphammer Mall a half-hour later, Paul reassured me that I looked twice as mean, and more brutish than ever. I felt great.

Every morning during our short stay in Ithaca, the lightweight straight-four challenged us on the lake. Except for an occasional piece, only their puddles scooting past our boat relayed their position. Over the next two weeks, I could sense that our speed was improving as the lightweight's puddles became sharper, which meant they were not as far ahead.

A few days into the camp, Tony Johnson cut four men, reducing his squad to only two four-with's. These two boats were much faster than the three boats we raced the first day. If our strength or resolve lagged for three consecutive strokes, Paul and I saw the immediate loss of a length to either the straight-four or one of the four-with's.

One day Tony asked why I had done so poorly at Harry's camp.

"I couldn't win any seat races," I told him. "It's that simple. I can offer a lot of excuses. I was tired from the single trials, the boatings were screwy. But when it came time for Harry to make his decision, he went with the proven seat racers."

"Would you rather be in Lucerne?" Tony asked.

"Nah, I'm having more fun here."

Tony laughed, but I was serious. Our training, the coaches, and especially the other rowers, all helped to make Ithaca an unexpected haven. Tony's college rowers had yet to develop the enormous egos, so common to elite athletes. His oarsmen still approached rowing as a medium of physical expression. They sought the sensation of powering a boat over the water using only their strength and endurance. For them, rowing was more than a means of acquiring a pair of national team shorts.

A frantic cloud had hung over Harry's camp. Every stroke, especially mine, had been a flawed, misdirected effort. The scullers in Hanover had not been interested in making the fastest boats, but in making the Olympic team. The distinction between the two is subtle - a point of view, an attitude. Now that Paul and I were on our own, we could pursue both goals, making the team and making the fastest boat, without conflict or interference.

In Ithaca the rhythm of the days was easy. I inevitably woke at 5:00 A.M., when the morning sun streamed through the boathouse windows, bounced off the lockers, and straight into my eyes. The instant I awoke, I was ready to go, but I still had two hours until practice. After a few days, I formed a routine that lasted for the duration of our stay. Every morning I drove to Mister Donut and sat with the old men who were drinking coffee and reading the local newspaper.

We were all refugees from a bad night's sleep, chased by challenges never satisfied, either in the past or in the future. My challenge awaited me. I was hungry for the show to begin. I never understood how Paul could sleep so late. Perhaps my internal clock was wound a bit tighter. For whatever reason, I was easy to find in the early dawn hours - sitting with the old men, drinking coffee, and hurrying the clock on its way.

I used the mornings to think, to conspire, to create new tricks. I loved to invent wild schemes and resurrect old devices for the sole purpose of furthering our mission. How could we flatten those guys at the trials? Maybe I'd cancel their hotel reservations in Princeton. No, too obvious. We needed more speed. We needed to row better. What if we encountered rough water at the trials? We'd better be prepared for anything. I had a dozen different on-the-water drills for perfecting our boatmanship. I wanted to be able to row our boat while standing on our heads.

Not often can a man apply himself wholeheartedly to a goal without the burden of family or money or some other real life distraction. It's good therapy. I recommend it.

My vision for those few weeks was flawless. I had the instincts of a hungry shark. I was living evolution, from boy to man to shark. The whole progression had taken about a dozen years, each step somehow tied to the rowing arena. For as long as I could remember, even before I started rowing, I possessed unlimited energy. For the last few years, this energy had been trapped in the form of an ill-defined, powerful anger. Fortunately, my passion for rowing had given this anger a constructive outlet.

Other motivational forces were at play-fear and love and ego. Below those forces were others, no doubt, forces I couldn't even identify much less admit to myself. But these only complemented my main source of fuel, hot anger. In the back-yard at my parent's house, I installed a boxing speed bag and a heavy bag. On those days when I couldn't flush the anger from my being by rowing or lifting weights, I pounded those bags until my knuckles bled. I had worn out two speed bags since Christmas of 1982.

Occasionally, I looked for the reasons behind my anger. Perhaps it simply came from the sport of rowing, which had kept me hostage for so many years. Often, I was angry at myself for getting old. Some nights, I sat on the edge of my bed and listened to my sore back begging for a rest. No, I had to ignore that reality. Not older, but stronger, better, tougher, meaner. I felt anger toward my opponents who mocked me as I passed them on the course. But rather than dwell on the reasons, I preferred to ride the anger like a surfer on a wave. I wanted to ride it to the very end of the universe.

Harry's camp had opened up a whole new vein of anger - a five-week nightmare. Harry wanted consistency? I'd show him the most consistent, crushing strokes he had ever seen.

20

MIKE LIVINGSTON, GURU ESQ.
TUESDAY, JUNE 12, 1984

BREAKFAST IN ITHACA WAS A SPECIAL PLEASURE. WE ATE IN Willard Straight, the Cornell students dining hall. For Tony's rowing team, which included Paul and myself as members in good standing, Willard Straight became food heaven.

Every oarsman, excluding unlucky lightweights, is committed to proving Stalin's famous line, 'Quantity is quality.' Rowers have complete license to eat everything: bagels with cream cheese, french fries, meat and eggs and whole milk, double-dipped chocolate donuts, soda and Cheetos. I discovered Buffalo-style chicken wings in Ithaca, and my taste buds have never been the same. Even if I had known about the evils of cholesterol, I wouldn't have cared. I wanted mega-calories, in any form. Between 1974 and 1984, I consumed 4000 calories a day, and my weight never budged from 194 pounds. Rowing and food are wonderfully inseparable.

Betty, the fry cook behind the counter, had a mocking, generally amused manner with the rowers. She loved the way we devoured her offerings. She did not take kindly, however, to our habit of trudging into her domain wearing wet rowing clothes, only moments before she had intended to close the grill. Betty made exceptionally good triple-cheese omelets, but the order had to come quickly: "Cheddar or Swiss, What'll it be? Cheddar or Swiss?" Failure to answer in the next milli-second resulted in a cheddar cheese omelet, that flavor of cheese being closest to her free hand.

I piled every inch of my tray with pancakes, fruit, yogurt, cereal, along with juice, coffee, and milk to lubricate the mess. Unfortunately, we were allowed just one trip through the buffet line, with no second helping. Even in the Olympics, an oarsmen is allowed a second chance if he false starts.

On our second day in Ithaca, I sat across from Paul at breakfast. Toward the end of our third course, I took a 30-minute audio cassette from my bag and slid it across the table. "Why don't you give it a listen when you have a minute?" I said. "I think you'll like it."

Paul read the name on the cassette: "Mike Livingston."

Mike Livingston changed my life.

Mike was tall, lean, strong, a rock climber's body, full beard, blond hair. He stood straight, with the posture of a confident man who had weathered many storms. The Livingston name was legendary in American rowing, and Mike was the corner-stone of that legend. He had rowed at Harvard under Harry's whip. During his first year out of college, he competed in the '72 Munich Olympics. Mike rowed in the bow seat of the eight-oared shell, the most difficult position. He was one of the lightest men in the boat, and by general consensus, also the toughest. The U.S. eight, with his brother Cleve rowing in the two-seat, performed an unexpected feat. The team won the silver medal. The New Zealand team, in a class by itself, won the gold, while the highly rated East Germans finished third, only a few inches behind the Americans.

Mike later became the rowing coach at the University of California, Berkeley. Through all my rowing years, I had never met Mike Livingston, which was strange because I knew almost everyone in the sport, from novice to Olympian. In 1983, Mike quit the Berkeley crew to practice law, or at least that was the reason I heard. Later I found out the real reason, he felt constrained by the limitations and bureaucracy inherent in an intercollegiate athletic program.

In early 1984, I did not have a coach. Mike Livingston, Olympic medalist, master of the struggle to succeed, did not have any students.

Actually, Mike had a few students. A Bay area rowing club, the Dirty Dozen, had hired him to be its coach. When the Dozen traveled to Newport Beach in February for a few weeks of intensive practice, I was introduced to the Guru.

Over the next two weeks, Mike read my training journal. He listened as I described my weight workouts. He watched me row. On the eve of his departure, Mike gave me a few private words, a slight restructuring in the way I approached my racing, and I was never the same.

Three rules made up the essence of his message:

First, "you must approach each test with the seriousness and passion that you would use to prepare to challenge your death. You must prepare - not to die - but to battle for your life in each moment, with every faculty and power available to you."

When compared to the ordinary concept of winning and losing, 'battling for my life' required a whole different level of consciousness. Mike's words reassured me that I was right to be obsessed, to train as if nothing else mattered. I had no interest in becoming rich and famous, or entering medical school, or any future beyond rowing. I only cared about preparing to be the best rower, with every faculty and power available to me.

Second, "you must purge yourself of all thoughts of self-importance and all inclination to judge either yourself or others. You must go to power with humility and deep respect."

Humility. Where the hell does humility come from? I've known people who've trained a dozen years, through a hundred wins and losses, and yet they were no more humble than a college freshman who has just won the Western Sprints. For some of us, humility does not come easily. A conscious effort has to be made to go after humility, to maintain respect for coaches and other scullers, along with various helpers, spectators, and even more prejudiced onlookers. I worked at maintaining respect and humility, with moderate success.

At the opposite end of the spectrum is pride, a nasty monkey for an athlete, or anyone for that matter, to carry on his back. Pride, according to *Websters*, is 'an overly high opinion of oneself. Haughtiness; arrogance.' Stay with humility. It will serve you well.

Finally Mike said, "you must assume full responsibility for choosing to pursue power. Know that you alone have chosen to be tested, and then proceed without doubt, remorse, or blame. You alone are responsible."

Tough rule. By following this rule, I had to abandon all the usual excuses. According to Mike, I was totally responsible for any results, including the single trials, the camp, the future. 'Taking complete responsibility' is the premiere rule for rowing, sports, life.

I had nearly mastered Mike's rules by the single trials. At Harry's camp I put away the rules. I suppose I felt far removed from the process of winning. Other rules took precedence - Harry's rules. In Ithaca I started at the beginning.

First, I gave Paul a copy of the audio tape that Mike had created for the Dirty Dozen. Since the tape was made for sweep rowers, Mike occasionally referred to eight-oared rowing, instead of sculling, but the essence of his message came through with undiminished power.

"Good day. We are privileged to live another day in this magnificent world. Today you will be tested."

Those opening lines from Mike's tape inevitably produced a change in my psyche, as if a drug had been injected straight into the center of my soul. One solitary word - tested - seemed to be directed only at me. It conjured up images of sweat running down my face, my legs on fire, the last ten strokes of a close, bitter race, my oars bending powerfully, strong to the last stroke. Today, every day, I will be tested.

Eventually, I knew every line, as though I was reading from a script. Not once during the several hundred listenings did I fall asleep. That alone was a miracle.

Very few people know how to win. And for some reason, most winners have a difficult time verbalizing the exact path they followed to accomplish their task. Mike is the rarest of men: he is a champion, and he knows precisely how to win. He told me these secrets in an impeccable manner.

21

A FEW DAYS AFTER WE ARRIVED IN ITHACA, I DROVE TO
Woolworth's Department Store and bought two closet-sized
mirrors, $9.95 each. They were four feet tall, a foot wide, smartly
framed in plastic-wood, marked down from $11.95.

Obviously a bargain, but why, in a store full of fine
appliances, cosmetics, and die-hard batteries, did I purchase
two mirrors? A cheap mirror is the poor man's video camera.
Actually, I preferred using mirrors. The feedback was
immediate, changes were visible instantly, and the mirrors cost
quite a bit less.

"Have you ever heard of mental imagery?" I asked Paul.

"Nope."

"Then you're in for a treat."

I proceeded to show my curious partner the Ways of
Shadow Rowing.

First, I must pay tribute to my teachers. While watching
an ABC Up-Close and Personal segment during the '80
Winter Olympics, I saw Eric Heiden practicing speed skating

151

in the basement of his house. He slid back and forth on a smooth piece of plywood, in front of a mirror. The commentator said Eric was working on his skating technique.

Four years later, on the same television show, I saw the Mahre twins, gold and silver medalists in slalom skiing, using a pre-race imagery drill before the start of their race. With eyes closed, they angled their hands back and forth in quick movements. Their hands represented skis, and each angled turn matched a turn on the racecourse.

I borrowed from Heiden, using his off-the-ice technical practice, and I borrowed from the Mahre's, using their pre-race imagery. I called my version Shadow Rowing.

After dinner each evening, Paul and I returned to the boat-house for one last workout. We arranged two rowing ergometers so that the machines overlapped, one slightly behind the other. The ergometers had big wheels, finely oiled chains, wooden handles - very sophisticated. But we left that gear alone. Our only accessories were the two mirrors, one in front of each machine. Paul sat in the stroke position. I sat in the bow position - exactly as in our double. Then we rowed the whole stroke cycle in pantomime.

From the first pseudo-stroke, our bizarre movements brought forth howls of laughter from the other rowers, the coaches, even Charlie the dog. After a few false starts, deciding we looked too silly to continue, then deciding we'd look even sillier if we lost the double trials, we pantomimed a complete race.

I set my stopwatch to the countdown mode - seven minutes - and pressed the start button. For 30 seconds we sat in the exact pre-race position, bodies tilted forward, arms outstretched, three-quarters of the way up the slide. When my watch hit 6:30, (a good time for 2000 meters), I said "Partez."

Not surprisingly, our rating was phenomenally high in the first 20 strokes, as we zipped up and down the slide, unencumbered by water resistance.

After 20 strokes, we shifted to 36 strokes a minute, a furious stroke rate when attempted on the water, but only slightly taxing using our current method. For the next six minutes, as my watch counted down to zero, we raced Charlie and Joe, the Hansen Brothers, Heppner and Lange, and anyone else I had ever dreamed of defeating. The mirrors kept us honest. Paul could see my actions. I could see his facial expressions. The slightest sign of distraction, by either of us, was immediately evident. As expected, in that first of several hundred efforts, we won. Hurray for us! Champions in our own imaginations.

Eventually, we developed a dozen different race scenarios: leading from the first stroke, trailing until the last stroke, and my favorite, hitting a buoy, losing an oar, and then having to recover in time to catch up and win the race. Throughout these scenarios we always maintained one common thread - intense, unyielding concentration.

My sister, Valerie, stopped in Ithaca for a few days to take a brief rest from her cross-country adventure. She was celebrating her graduation from college by touring the U.S. in her old Vega, with only her dog Cameo and a .38 Smith & Wesson for company. I recruited Val to be *The Distracter*.

Val's mission was to make us look away from the mirrors, and she threw herself into the task with complete abandon - jumping around, screaming, dumping water on us. Any action was legal. Once Valerie even read from one of her Harlequins: "She thrust her body close to her lover's chest, and with squeals of pain and delight she lowered herself onto..." Pure concentration, eyes glued to the mirror. Paul and I sought flawless technique, powerful rhythm, and cool control, all within the heat of passion.

Our shadow races overcame several problems. We didn't have enough time before the Olympic trials to attempt a real 2000-meter race - that would have been too tiring. Still, to be fully prepared, we should have had a dozen such races. The shadow drill filled in the missing races, and without totally exhausting us.

A real 2000-meter race, such as we imitated during shadow rowing, is a peculiar nightmare. Some rowers, renowned weight room studs, have suddenly found themselves lacking the strength to sit upright on the starting line. A race is like a test in school. A semester's worth of studying is no guarantee that your mind won't go blank once the exam in placed in front of you.

And always, in an important race like the Olympic trials, a few hundred doubts and distractions try to destroy your confidence. Sturdy boats and oars, which have withstood months of hard labor, suddenly seem as fragile as eggshells. Race officials roar around in their smelly launches, making wakes, issuing orders, adding to the confusion. The worse distraction is the common delay-of-race, from five minutes to five hours. These periods of complete inactivity are never rehearsed in a practice session, and they can totally dissolve one's pre-race mentality. Paul and I practiced every aspect - even waiting at the starting line.

A man goes through many changes in 2000 meters. Some are not very pretty. Some make you hate yourself. Some make you wonder if you've been rowing for only three or four days. To avoid that fate, we prepared for all possibilities. If a meteor landed ten feet off our stern, we would not blink. Paul and I would be aware, yet impassive to the outside world. Every ounce of energy would be funneled into the water and not wasted by looking around, worrying about our opponents, wondering about things that didn't concern our primary goal - to be first across the finish line. We had a big task, for which we needed only the simplest of tools, two mirrors.

While Charlie and Joe competed in Lucerne against the best double scullers in the world, Paul and I fought our battles in a darkened corner of the Cornell boathouse.

Paul willingly tried my little gimmicks, shadow rowing, endless on-the-water drills, three and four workouts a day. He wasn't sure I knew what I was doing, but he didn't squawk, and he always gave his best effort. I knew what I was doing. I was a crazed man using the sanest techniques. I had spent a lifetime preparing for these few weeks, and I knew exactly how to use each hour. The feeling was exquisite.

Our partnership worked, not by luck, but by intense practice, a little creativity, and total cooperation in pursuit of our common goal.

22

DISPATCH FROM LUCERNE
5:50 P.M., MONDAY, JUNE 18, 1984

"HEY BRAD, I'VE GOT BIGGY ON THE PHONE," PAUL SAID. "DO
you want to talk to him?"

"No. Not really," I said. "Just ask him about Lucerne."

Harry and his boys were back from Lucerne and I was
dying to know the results. I had predicted the quad, with Jack
Frackleton rowing in the bow seat, would not make the
finals. With Tiff, however, I thought the quad might make the
finals and eventually finish in fifth or sixth place. The double
scull was a different matter. I prayed for Charlie and Joe not
to make the finals on either day.

"You're never going to believe this," Paul said, hanging up
the phone, "but with Jack, the quad made the finals and
finished third. With Tiff, they didn't even make the finals."

Bad news.

"Well, how about the double?" I asked.

"Charlie and Joe did pretty well."

"How well?"

"They finished fifth on Saturday and fourth on Sunday."

"Oh."

Very bad news.

In Lucerne, the Love Boat, one of the more civil nicknames I had given the Charlie Altekruse-Joe Bouscaren
combination, had defeated some of the best crews in the world.
Charlie and Joe would be sky high after their performance.
Our task had gone from being difficult to being nearly
impossible.

The quad results were almost more discouraging. Bracken's
quad, with Tiff in the bow, had completely failed on Saturday. In their heat, they finished four lengths behind the
winner. On Sunday, with Frackleton instead of Tiff, Bracken's
quad was transformed into a world-class contender. They made
the finals, which was good, and finished third, which was
amazing. An American quadruple scull had never won a medal
in an international regatta, until Sunday.

What the hell was going on? I had rowed in Bracken's
quad. I knew its ability. Somewhere along the line they
improved about 100 percent. But why had it gone worse with
Tiff? I still had a lot to learn about the sport of sculling.

Biggy also raced in Lucerne. More bad news. He failed to
make the finals on either day. Ouch. I raced with Biggy, at
least in spirit. His victories were mine, and so were his defeats.
I wanted to be reassured that I had been a world-class single
sculler on the day of the Olympic trials. Damn him for going
slow.

Harry's squad returned to Hanover for its final tune-up
before the trials - ten days away - and within a few hours of
settling in, the rumor mill began to churn. First off, Tiff and
Biggy raced a double scull against the Love Boat. Without
having practiced, and using a slower boat, Tiff and Biggy
defeated Charlie and Joe by half a length.

A tempting thought immediately formed in Biggy's head: if he won the double trials with Tiff, a medal at the Olympics was possible. Tiff was overjoyed at the thought of racing the double with Biggy. Jack Frackleton was firmly in the bow seat of the quad, and not even another day of seat racing in Hanover could work in Tiff's favor.

Joe and Biggy, both former Yale oarsmen, both future doctors and best of friends, had roomed together upon returning to Hanover from Lucerne. But immediately following that fateful practice, Joe had packed his clothes and moved into a different room. I danced when I heard that news. A moderate level of unrest had reached Hanover - yes, good, excellent. A sharp thorn had lodged in the backside of their concentration.

Unfortunately, Harry soon stepped into the fray. He entered Biggy's room and closed the door, an act very similar to one that I had experienced not long before. When Harry emerged, Biggy was firmly in the single, and Tiff was on his own.

For over a decade, Tiff's loyalty to Harry had worked well for both parties. Yet for some reason, this summer was different. Perhaps if Harry had believed in Tiff's abilities, things might have gone better. Tiff needed time to make the difficult transition from the single scull to the quad. With a few hundred miles of unpressured rowing, a week or ten days perhaps, Tiff could have resumed his roll as the team's prime boat mover, and equally important, as the team leader.

Tiff had no choice but to leave Hanover in search of a new partner. He packed his bags one last time, and then made a few phone calls. His first call was to me.

"Tiff, it's good to hear your voice," I said.

"I figure you know why I'm calling," he said. "Do you want to row the double with me?"

I took a deep breath, thought for a long moment, and then said, "Sorry, Tiff, I can't do it."

"Then I'll see you at the double trials," Tiff said, hanging up before I could reply. I felt sick as I put down the phone. Why hadn't Tiff and I joined forces the day we lost the single trials? We had plenty of time to strike a bargain while waiting in the USOC drug testing lab.

And now, with a simple 'Yes,' I could have had a sleek, Ivy League partner, a champion on every level, instead of a balding fisherman from Washington State University. But I couldn't do it. I had given my word to Paul. I had to fulfill the promise we made on the porch of the Harvard Boathouse. The single scull had been so simple in comparison - you made promises only to yourself. I told Paul of my conversation with Tiff, and once again we shook hands on our partnership.

Tiff wasted no time in calling Jim Dietz with his offer. Like me, Dietz already had a partner, my old training buddy, Dan Louis. Only a few words were needed, "Hi Jim, this is Tiff," for Dietz to toss Dan overboard. Loyalty to Dan was not worth passing up the third best sculler in the world, at least not for Dietz. Dan was a good sculler, but Tiff was a great sculler, and with only a few days until the trials, Dietz went with the proven man.

The summer's most pathetic event took place after Tiff spoke with Dietz. Tiff asked Harry for permission to use one of the many double sculls that were sitting on the trailer, blistering under the Hanover sun. Harry's answer was final and emphatic. "No. Find your own boat."

Wow. When I heard what had happened, I couldn't believe it. Yes, it was true. Harry and Tiff, ten years together, finished in a blink. I felt great pain for Tiff. He could have left long ago, but instead he stayed loyal to Harry. Athletes do crazy things during the Olympic year, and I suppose the same could be said for coaches. Before Harry's words had stopped echoing in the pine trees, Tiff was speeding to Boston at 90 miles an hour.

Tiff soon found another boat. The Cromwell double, which had been damaged the first day of Harry's camp, was now repaired and ready to race. Gail Cromwell had been leery of Harry Parker before the accident, and now she cursed like a longshoreman at the mention of his name. If Tiff and Dietz could defeat Harry's Love Boat, her prayers would be answered. I doubt if Tiff mentioned to Gail that he had been rowing in the bow seat, the steering position, when the Cromwell double had nearly sunk. The next morning, Tiff drove to the New York Athletic Club's Orchard Beach boat-house with the Cromwell double strapped to the roof of his Turbo Saab.

Tiff and Dietz had little time to waste. Only five days remained until the first heat of the Olympic double scull trials.

Even with their limited practice, I feared this new challenge even more than the Love Boat. Paul and I spent a few minutes counting the combined trial wins for Tiff and Dietz. We counted an astonishing 26 victories.

"And don't forget 1967," Tony Johnson said, as he walked past. "Dietz was the youth sculler that year. He won the gold medal in the single scull at the Junior World Rowing Championships."

Paul and I counted our combined trial victories on one hand.

"To Hell with them," I said. "I don't care who we race. Charlie and Joe, Tiff and Dietz, it doesn't matter. We'll rip their nuts off and stuff them down their throats."

I encouraged any words, any action that raised our level of intensity as the day of judgment drew near.

My life was going to end in a few days. I wasn't a future doctor. I wasn't a future anything. My life consisted of a solitary race, now only five days away, and I wanted to make sure that I went out in a flaming, hell-bent explosion.

23

GRIP BAPTISM
JUNE 21, 1984

ABOUT A WEEK BEFORE THE TRIALS, I DECIDED TO CHANGE MY grips. Traumatic business, grip changing, but the time had arrived. My grips had worn smooth and lost their stickiness, and the wooden handles underneath were beginning to show through in places.

Deep troughs had formed where my fingers had latched onto the oars. My personality was worn into the rubber. Needless to say, I'd grown attached to these grips, which made the parting all the more difficult. But I wanted new rubber under my hands - new blood to squeeze from my handles. The timing had to be just right - not too soon before the trials, not too late. Today, full moon, high tide, Venus aligned with Mars, full tank of gas, was just right.

I bought my grips directly from the manufacturer, Stampfli Boatbuilders of Zurich, and when they arrived in the mail, I could smell the sweet orange rubber even before I opened the box. In size and shape, a grip resembled a rigid condom, except it has a small hole in the rounded end. The rubber was about an eighth-inch thick, with delicate knurling along the outer skin. Inscribed in fine lettering, at the very base of each grip, were the words, 'Staempfliboats Zurich.'

Early in my rowing career, I learned a good rule: NEVER LET YOUR GRIPS TOUCH THE GROUND.

Rowing shorts cushioned my buttocks against the seat, socks protected my feet. The sole point of contact between my body and the equipment were my hands choking the grips. For over a decade, my hands had been a combination of raw blisters and hardened calluses. Through the years I had acquired some proficiency as a surgeon, slicing open the blisters with a flame-sterilized, single-sided razor and using that same razor to shave the calluses. Sometimes a blister would burst open in the middle of a workout, and I'd feel the cool juice spreading over my hand. I kept my grips clean because I couldn't risk losing a week or two of practice with infected hands, the result of having rowed with a pair of soiled grips.

I cut away the old grips with a sharp knife and tossed them aside. Now for the baptism. With the hose at my feet, water trickling out, I braced the port oar against the wall of the boathouse. I wedged the new grip onto the end of the bare wooden handle, then placed the hose over the end of the grip. With my free hand, I made a tight seal where the grip met the handle. As the water pressure gradually increased, the grip inflated like a balloon. At the right instant - and only years of practice dictated that instant - I released my right hand. Water squirted in every direction, most of it into my face, as the grip scooted down the shaft, instantly securing itself to the wooden handle as if welded into place.

My rowing career began as wooden boats and oars were being replaced by plastic replicas. These rubber grips were the last vestiges of the old way of rowing, at least in regard to equipment. Although I used a plastic boat for racing, I had not forsaken my rowing roots. Stowed in the eves of my father's garage was my first racing boat, a beautiful wooden Pocock single scull. I had purchased the boat in 1976, from the Men's Olympic Rowing Committee; the deal was finalized a few days before the closing ceremonies at the Montreal Olympics.

A problem soon arose. The Committee's agent, Jack Frailey, with whom I had arranged the purchase, had apparently acted without the authorization of the Committee. A few weeks after I received my boat, he suddenly informed me that it had to be returned. With the support of my father, and after consulting a lawyer to make sure that I was the legal owner, I told Jack to buzz off. That hassle went on for years.

Nothing came easy in my rowing career, but fortunately I had a deep passion for sculling, and my family provided incalculable support. Equally important, a few special people assisted me on my journey.

Summer 1977: I experienced the most unexpected blessing. For a few weeks, I trained with my original sculling hero, the great Irishman, Sean Drea. I met Sean in Philadelphia, his adopted hometown, and we rowed side by side on the Schuylkill River. At the 4th of July Regatta that year, we both won the single scull event in our respective categories, elite and senior. To the victors went a wristwatch, inscribed with the date and the event. My new prize was exactly like Sean's, except that the inscription on his watch read, 'Elite Single.'

Sean rowed with an upright style and high rating. His blade work, even at 40 strokes a minutes, was flawless. In some ways he was the rowing equivalent of my carpenter mentor, Carl Hilterbrand. Sean looked more like a boxer than a sculler, thick-chested, huge wrists and forearms. Anyone who has the good fortune to have watched Sean row, or better yet, to have known this classy, unselfish champion, possesses a memory to be treasured.

Ten years before, I had read a magazine article about Sean in *The Oarsmen*, titled, 'Climbing the Ladder of Success.' I still had that article, and I looked at it now and again. Sean's rise to sculling greatness had been painfully slow, but he was relentless. Finally he reached the top, including a place in the Guinness Book of Records for having rowed the fastest 2000 meters ever recorded in Olympic competition, 6:52.46, in a preliminary race at the '76 Montreal Olympics. His greatest success was at the Henley Royal Regatta, where he won the single sculls event, known as the Diamond Challenge Sculls, three times.

I had wanted to emulate Sean from the moment I read the article. My goal still hadn't changed, although at times it seemed as though the rungs on my own ladder of success were miles apart.

After a promising start in 1977, I injured my leg in '78. In 1979, I toured Europe on a self-guided, self-funded study of the rowing world, racing the single scull in several international regattas and making the finals in almost every one. I learned a few secrets during the tour. For instance, the best scullers are fast all season long, and not only at the World Championships. I also had a great time, especially when I trained at the Spanish national rowing camp, located in Banyoles. I was the only American to have ever rowed at this unique training camp.

One day the head coach, Thor Nilsen, watched me row a few strokes. Then he said to his assistant coach, Jens MacMaren, "That American will never be a champion."

After relaying Thor's critique, Jens MacMaren, who hated Thor Nilsen, said to me, "That almost certainly means you will be a champion."

When I returned from Europe, I attended the national team sculling camp, from which the quad, destined to compete in the '79 World Championships, would be selected. I performed well, but the coach, the Harvard lightweight coach at the time, selected a Harvard sculler instead of me. That marked the first time I felt I was discriminated against based on the college that I had attended.

In 1980, the Olympic sculling coach, a different man, suggested that I not bother coming to his Florida training camp. In no uncertain terms, he told me I'd be wasting my time. Following my usual course of action, I disagreed, paid my own way to Florida, and crashed his Tampa training party. I promptly won all my seat races. The coach had no choice but to put me in the quad.

The next year, 1981, I was thoroughly primed to become the top single sculler in the country, only to have a strange character named John Biglow overwhelm the U.S. sculling scene. Biggy claimed the single for his own in '81, and he retained it the following year.

In the summer of '82, I raced in an all-star quad at the trials. We only practiced once or twice, but we were so good, so confident, that each of us predicted an easy victory. Our only challenge was from a Philadelphia club quad, which happened to be stroked by Charlie Bracken, with Jack Frackleton in the two seat. At the trials, the all-stars, Tiff, Jim Dietz, Sean Colgan, and I, suddenly became candidates for the all-slow team. We lost by eight seconds to the club boat.

From year to year, the characters in my rowing career, never changed very much. Only the boatings were reshuffled.

Over the last decade, a pattern had been established: I had made the national rowing team every three years, '77, '80, '83. If history was any indicator, I wouldn't make another national team again until 1986. To Hell with preordained patterns. The challenge that was torturing me had to be solved today, this minute, this Olympiad, 1-9-8-4.

24

IN SEARCH OF A NEW CHARIOT
FRIDAY, JUNE 22, 1984

ONE CRITICAL PART OF OUR PLAN CAUSED ME WORRY. THE Carbocraft that we had freed from Harry's grasp was adequate for training, but we needed a special boat to win the trials, something light and stiff, racy hull design, two-tone paint job, chrome-plated riggers.

Our Carbocraft had none of these characteristics.

Nonetheless, I still had a deep affection for her. When I'd tried out for the '80 Olympic team, I won my important seat races in this boat. The Carbocraft, or 'Carbo,' was brand new that year, and she raced fast and straight every time I stepped into her. Since then quite a few thousand miles had passed beneath the hull of this grey war ship. Her honeycomb skin had soaked up a few gallons of water along the way. Her riggers had broken and been re-welded a half-dozen times.

Officially, the Carbo belonged to the Men's Olympic Rowing Committee, but it had resided in the Harvard Boathouse for so long that I worried that Harry might try to recover his assumed property when we arrived at the trials. The best solution was a new chariot.

My old training partner, Dan Louis, owned the best double scull in the country, and one of the few boats that Harry had not acquired for his camp. I placed a casual phone call to Dan, who had returned to Philadelphia after his brief fling with Jim Dietz.

Brad: "How's the weather?"

Dan: "Hot. Brutal. Humid as Hell."

Brad: "Bummer about Dietz."

Dan: "Yeah."

Brad: "To Hell with him. He showed himself to be little better than Harry by cutting you loose."

Dan: "Doesn't matter. He won't win the trials, even with Tiff. Dietz is out of shape."

Brad: "Say, by the way, I was wondering if I could rent your boat for a few days?"

Dan: "Hmm. Let me think about it."

Borrowing another man's boat is roughly the same as asking if he wouldn't mind if you took his little sister to Aspen for a weekend ski trip. Boats are special, delicate, to be cherished and protected at all costs. A good double scull is worth about $8,000, but during certain times of the year, and especially the Olympic year, they're worth well over a million dollars. I had called Dan at the most crucial time. He was looking for a new partner, and certainly he needed his own boat. As Paul and I drove to Philadelphia, the city of brotherly love, I kept thinking that I was asking a great deal of Dan, maybe too much.

Dan was training at the Vesper Boat Club, in the heart of Philadelphia's Boathouse Row. Vesper dated from the mid-1800s, a time when rowing was a wild sport, full of colorful practitioners, and the favorite betting pastime of gamblers. This grand era is neatly immortalized by the painter, Thomas

Eakins. His classic painting, *Turning the Stake*, shows how few changes in technique, equipment, or oarsmen have occurred over the last hundred years.

On either side of Vesper, a dozen equally venerable boathouses stood shoulder to shoulder, next to the grey-brown Schuylkill River. I've always thought that Boathouse Row looked best at night, when hundreds of electric lights outlined the shape of each building, turning them into fantastic postcard themes. I knew, however, from many visits to Boathouse Row, that at the same time, armies of rats were holding maneuvers in the basements.

Philadelphia, 1977. During my first summer of sculling, I lived in the Crescent Boathouse, on the downstream end of Boathouse Row. After the single trials, where I finished third - not bad for a first-year sculler - I joined a makeshift quad-crew. We were a diverse team: Ted Van Dusen (the well-known boat builder from Boston), Casey Baker from Florida, John Bannan of Vesper, and me, representing the Long Beach Rowing Association at the time.

We were coached by Gus Ignas, the toughest oarsman on the Schuylkill River in the late '60s.

About a week before we departed for the World Championships, I walked from Crescent to Vesper for our morning workout. A new greeting waited for me at Vesper's front door: "Private Club, Members Only, Keep Out." Someone had stenciled these words on every door and blank wall, both inside and out. The message was obviously directed towards Ted and me, since we did not belong to Vesper.

'Locals only' graffiti is a common sight in the surfing world, but I was surprised to see it in the genteel world of rowing. Philly boys, I came to learn that summer, loved their club to the point of obsession. And they disliked most outsiders.

Every summer for 11 years, I'd traveled to the East coast, 3,300 miles, three time zones. I often wished these Philly boys, who rarely left their immediate area code, would attempt a similar journey to the West coast. After sitting in a noisy car for three or four days, arriving exhausted, searching for a place to stay, a place to train, a part-time job, they might gain some insight into the challenge of relocating to the other side of the country.

At four in the afternoon, Paul and I parked in front of Vesper and unpeeled from the car. I had lost several pounds in perspiration during the trip, as if I'd run from Ithaca, instead of driven.

Dan walked up, and we shook hands for a long time. Dan and I were best friends and training partners, a rare combination that created a special bond between us. I am fortunate to have known Dan in both capacities.

Dan looked good. The sauna of this ordinary Philly summer did not allow him to wear his leather jacket, but otherwise he seemed happy.

"You and Paul have made a big hit here in Philly," he said. "You guys are heroes."

I thought he was joking, but over the next hour, we were greeted by a dozen rowers and coaches, all of whom wished us the best of luck in destroying the camp entry at the trials. In the days since our split from Harry, the story had changed a dozen times, growing in leaps and bounds, until Paul and I stood as the great hope against the dreaded camp system.

"You even have a nickname," Dan said. "Campbusters."

Boathouse Row was the home of club rowing, and it opposed any type of camp selection process. National team selection camps, both sweep and sculling, usually produced the best crews in the country. They also had the unfortunate side effect of drawing the best oarsmen away from the rowing clubs.

I soon felt uncomfortable, not only from the oppressive heat, but from receiving so much attention. One coach took me aside to convey a secret tip on how to beat Charlie Altekruse: "Just keep your hands moving at the finish, if you want to beat Charlie," he said in his thick German accent. "Keep the hands moving, and you will kill that turkey."

I nodded yes, but I never understood what he meant.

Finally, Dan and I talked business.

Brad: "Paul and I can win the trials with your boat. You'll have a better chance if you row in the quad trials. Get yourself a decent boat, and then wait until the double trials are over. You can pick and choose the three best guys to row in your quad."

Dan: "I've considered it. It might work."

Brad: "I tell you what. If we don't win the double trials, we'll row with you in the quad. Plus, I'll pay for the use of your double."

Dan: "Save your money."

Brad: "It's not mine. I'm planning to bill the U.S. Olympic Committee for all these costs, as soon as we win."

Dan: "Okay. How about $100?"

Brad: "I was thinking of $150. You boat's worth a hundred times that much - at least to me."

Dan: "Okay, deal. But be damn careful. I've spent the whole summer tuning her up. She's a rocket ship."

Dan was tough. He had more strength and endurance than anyone currently rowing in Harry's quad, and in my unsolicited opinion he would have been the perfect choice to stroke the boat. Dan rowed with a smooth, easy rhythm, and even in the heat of battle, he appeared to be hardly trying when actually he was giving everything to the effort. This 'hardly trying' facade, when the going is tough, is the essence of good rowing. He also had a few little quirks left over from his U.C. Berkeley crew days, which separated him from the boring pack. When the weather permitted, for example, Dan wore a 17-zipper Easy Rider leather jacket that I envied like hell until I got one of my own. I never did understand why Harry overlooked Dan as a candidate for sculling camp.

Driving home was pure torture. With Dan's boat tied onto the roof of our mini-Renault, I was instantly transformed into the world's slowest driver. Likewise, every truck seemed intent on tailgating us, missing the stern of our new double by inches.

The hardest part of the drive was the last 30 miles, Highway 79, two lanes, deserted, with real country dark leading the way.

The road dipped and turned as it led into Ithaca. Paul slept without a care, while I poured lukewarm water down my back to stay awake. The relief I felt when we pulled into the Cornell Boathouse parking lot, safe at last, was beyond words.

25

THE LAST HALCYON DAY
THURSDAY, JUNE 28, 1984

YOU ARE INVITED TO A FINAL ITHACA WORKOUT!

PLACE: STORM CHANNEL
TIME: 8:15 A.M.
CONTESTANTS:
   LIGHTWEIGHT STRAIGHT-FOUR
   TONY'S BEST FOUR-WITH COXSWAIN
   ENQUIST-LEWIS DOUBLE SCULL
WORKOUT: FOUR TIMES 500 METERS
RSVP: NOT NEEDED. WE KNOW YOU'LL BE THERE

Our goal was to beat the lightweights and the four-with.

More importantly, we wanted to row at least one of the 500-meter pieces in 1:30, one minute and thirty seconds, 90 seconds in total, not very long in the overall history of the planet - only the slimmest slice of life.

I figured that a world class double scull had to row four consecutive 1:35s, which translated into a 6:20, the winning time at the '82 World Championships on the flat-and-fast Lucerne course. A strong tailwind had interfered with the times

175

at the '83 Worlds, so we based our goal on the times recorded in '82.

If we could row one 500-meter piece in 1:30, I felt our speed would be unmatchable. Since arriving in Ithaca, we had rowed dozens of 500-meter pieces, the fastest being 1:32.2, but now we were tapered down, rested, with a faster boat, fired-up, pumped-up, two-cups-of-coffee ready to rock and roll.

Tony and Fin stood on the grassy embankment at the starting line, next to Tony's blue Yale van. Two or three impatient observers, lovers of good rowing theater, looked out the windows of the van, waiting for the show to begin. The storm channel was too skinny to accommodate three boats and a coaching launch, so Tony's van was called into action.

All three boats sat poised, waiting at attention, listening for the starting commands.

When ready, Tony said, "Double scull, prêt? Four-with, prêt? Lightweights, prêt? Etes vous prêt? Partez!"

Two strokes later he shouted, "Hold it! Hold it right there! Lewis, what are you guys doing? You left on the *Etes*."

"Sorry, we got excited."

"Yeah? Well, if you get excited at the trials, then you're going to get a false start. Let's try it again."

A minute later Tony yelled the magic word, and we swung into the first stroke.

Five hundred meters isn't far: 60 strokes, six *tens*. Some oarsmen claim that 500 meters is the hardest unit of effort - just long enough to knock you out. Certainly, the pain experienced in a max-effort 500 is different from that in a 2000-meter race. If done properly, a hard 500-meter piece will produce an unforgettable, brain-torching sensation. Even better than the pain are the strange thoughts that inevitably come spinning out of your consciousness in the middle of a 500.

I felt okay for the first 45 seconds, and then my vision grew fuzzy. My lungs felt like deflated balloons. I would have sucked oxygen through my ears, if that were possible. I was experiencing oxygen debt, or perhaps better stated, oxygen death.

We were rowing about 40 strokes a minute, five or six beats above our usual race rating. Our hands rifled away from our bodies at the finish of each stroke, and our blazing return up the slides assured me the rating was too high. It didn't matter. We were only going 500 meters. As soon as this workout is over, I thought, I'm going to get my own stroke meter. Paul had a stroke meter, but I had nothing to check our rating. It didn't matter. We were only going 500 meters.

I felt the ballast stowed in front of my feet shift slightly. Thanks to Dan, we now possessed a true rarity, a boat that weighed less than the FISA minimum of 26 kilos or 57.32 pounds. To make our boat legal we added seven pounds, in the form of lead tire weights stuffed into two socks. The ballast also provided a steadying effect during rough water outings.

Tony's van was moving slowly along the embankment. He had not sped up for the finish, so I knew we had at least 150 meters to go. Where was that damn white stick that marked the finish line? Some kid probably moved it last night. I would have preferred a neon sign, a billboard shouting: 'This is it - 500-meter finish line.'

The instant I saw the white stick over my shoulder, Tony's van raced ahead, so that they'd be on the finish line to get an accurate time.

"Last ten," I said to Paul.

Thirteen strokes later, Tony yelled, "Paddle."

"Listen up," Tony said, after we caught our breath. "Real close racing. Good rowing, guys. Fin and I call that piece a tie between the straight-four and the double. The four-with was a length back. Here's the time. I'm reading straight off the watch. No bullshitting here. The lightweights and double rowed 1:29.9. Nicely done."

Paul and I rowed the next 500 in 1:29.7. Records aren't kept for 500-meter times, but I had a feeling we had just rowed a couple of 500s that would hold their own against any double scull in the world. We were ready for the Love Boat, Tiff and Dietz, and anyone else who might show up. Bring on the Olympic trials.

After practice we loaded our double onto Tony's trailer in preparation for the trip to Princeton. When the last knot was tied, we stood with the lightweights, Tony's four-with, Erwin the rigger, Fin, Tony, all our new friends. This scene differed in every way from the Hanover boat loading party, with Harry and his boys. For once, I wanted a camp to continue. My world had changed remarkably fast, thanks to the gracious way they had accepted us from the first handshake. I felt lucky to have met such good people.

Tony and his dog, Rusty, entertained us with a new trick. Tony asked Rusty, "What do you want to do - go to Harvard or die? Harvard or die? What's it going to be, Rusty?"

Rusty remembered his part in the game and promptly rolled over and hung his paws in the air.

"Guess he'd rather die," Tony said with a grin.

26

COOLING OUT AT THE DOUBLE TRIALS
1:40 P.M., FRIDAY, JUNE 29, 1984

COOL. WE WERE COOL. TOO COOL? NEVER TOO COOL.

Our opponents had been melting in Princeton's torrid humidity since Wednesday, while we stayed nice and fresh in Ithaca until the last possible moment. Finally we coasted, cool and aloof as though our little Renault was a Rolls Royce limousine, out of the shadows and into the parking lot at the finish line of the Princeton racecourse.

Paul and I immediately went for a short row, four times 2000 meters at half-power, just to get the feel of the buoys and to stretch out after the drive. We had the whole hot humid afternoon to ourselves. Not another boat was on the racecourse, just the way we wanted it.

As we returned to the dock we agreed to stay just long enough to secure our boat to the trailer, and then we'd fade into the background. To avoid losing track of our purpose, so easy to do during pre-race socializing, I made up a special cool-rule: once we had shaken hands with five different people, we would immediately leave the premises.

179

After tying down our boat, we invoked the handshake rule. Within a few minutes, we had exhausted our supply of handshakes, and with a nod, we pulled back our feelers and started to leave the racecourse. As we drove along the bumpy parking lot toward the exit, Tiff and Dietz suddenly marched up to us, pointing and laughing, calling us Campbusters and other names, all in good fun. Only for Tiff and Dietz did we temporarily suspend the rule.

Paul and I jumped out of the car and greeted our allies. The four of us chatted like best friends, saying outrageous lies about Charlie and Joe, laughing at the strange rumors we had heard - fights, forced silence, boat switching, lawyers. At that moment, I formed a new cool-rule: to laugh on the eve of the Olympic trials, when the tension rendered most competitors grim and unsmiling, was super-cool.

"If we don't win," Dietz said in parting, "then I want you guys to win."

"Well, all right, same here," I replied, caught off guard by Dietz's blunt remark. Yes, a few allies might come in handy against Harry, the camp double, the camp quad, and anyone else who might have reason to wish us misfortune. The camp double was still heavily favored, and certainly after Lucerne they had every reason to expect an easy victory. But after hearing a few of the stories coming down from Hanover, I had to wonder if a small crack hadn't opened in the camp armor.

As we drove away, I laughed one last time. In the rear view mirror, I saw a dozen quick glances in our direction. Rowers are the master of the quick glance. They want to look, but they don't want to be caught in the act. When a couple of *isolantoes*, Paul and I, showed up in full battle regalia, acting cool and confident, I suppose we gave observers plenty of reason to look.

Driving toward Princeton's hotel circle, the choice of accommodations suddenly became a problem. Paul wanted to stay at the Scanticon Hotel while I insisted on my old haunt, the secluded Ramada Inn.

"Listen Paul. This is important. We don't want to be within a mile of that place. You'll be tripping over a camp guy every time you step out of the bathroom."

"But I can't afford the Ramada, and besides, I'll spend all my time at the Scanticon anyway. My Mom and girlfriend are staying there."

"So is the rest of the world, including the Love Boat, Tiff and Dietz, Curtis's quad, Bracken's quad, and the guy we want to avoid the most, Harry Parker."

In order to maintain our good relationship, I gave in to Paul's argument, and we drove toward the Scanticon. About 400 yards from the hotel, we became locked in a traffic jam, and for the next five minutes, we barely moved.

"Paul, you could be taking a nap right now if we were staying at the Ramada. What do say you? Ramada, yes?"

"Well, okay, but you'll have to lend me some money."

"To hell with the money, we're on a mission."

At the single trials, I had wanted to avoid Harry due to some vague feelings of uneasiness on my part. Now those feelings had a razor sharp edge. A quick u-turn, and three miles later we stood at the Ramadas check-in desk.

I immediately noticed that we were not the only Olympic hopefuls-in-residence. Mike Livingston's rowing club, the Dirty Dozen, had just returned from a European regatta tour, and now they were staying at the Ramada in anticipation of the Olympic four-with coxswain trials.

Later in the evening, I sat across from Mike in the hotel's restaurant.

"How was your world tour?" I asked him.

"First class," Mike said. "Everything was top of the line. We had a few problems, as you'd expect."

"Yeah? Like what?"

"Well, Brad, the Doz were racing over their heads. We hit every major international regatta, and in many, the Doz lined up against national teams - the fastest crews in the world. Not surprisingly, the Doz lost most of their races. For the first time, I think, the men understood just how fast the competition is at the summit. For some, that was a devastating realization. For others, it only raised their level of commitment and sharpened their focus. But as you well know, losing is no fun, and they did more than their share. But enough about the Doz. I want to know how you're doing."

For the next 15 minutes, I told Mike about my roller coaster summer. He was especially interested in my problems at the sculling camp because Harry Parker had been Mike's coach at Harvard and later for the '72 Olympic eight.

After relating the unabridged story, Mike took a deep breath and said, "You know, Brad, you're a very smart young man."

"You're kidding."

"No, I'm not. I'm sure you made the right move by quitting Harry's camp. You and Paul should easily win the trials."

I laughed when he said that, so matter-of-factly, as if we were racing in the Long Beach Christmas Regatta.

"The Olympics will be harder," he continued, "but I've seen the best doubles in Europe, and you can beat them."

He leaned closer: "Listen carefully. If you'd won the single trials, your chance of winning a gold medal at the Olympics would be very small. Kolbe and Karppinen are in a class by themselves. At best, you'd be fighting for a bronze medal. The double is the perfect boat for you. It's wide open. You don't need to change a thing to beat Charlie and Joe. After you win the trials, we'll spend a few hours together and straighten out any problems."

Mike wrote his phone number on a corner of the placemat, tore it off, and handed it to me. "Call me after you win."

The next morning Paul and I raced our heat. Seventeen doubles had entered the trials, three heats, winners advancing to the finals, losers to the afternoon's repêchage.

We had an easy draw and a good start. After ten strokes, we led by a boat length. We won by six lengths of open water.

In the evening Paul went to dinner with his girlfriend, while I stayed in the room. I had a lot of energy. I was antsy, restless. Our tapering down had been just right - I was ready to jump out the window.

I spent a portion of my nervous energy creating a sign. Using an old tarp and a can of spray paint, I wrote in huge letters: NOBODY BEATS US!

More than simply a positive ideal, 'Nobody Beats Us!' served as our main 'trigger.' During our shadow races, we practiced using trigger words, private verbal keys that unlocked certain thoughts for us. We had a half-dozen phrases - some dealt with maintaining our technique, two dealt with our stroke rating.

The most powerful phrase was 'Nobody Beats Us!' According to our plan, when I said these words to Paul toward the end of the race, we would immediately shift into our final sprint, rowing as high and hard as possible, straight through, until we crossed the finish line.

I hung the immense tarp on the wall in front of our beds, just to make sure, in all the excitement, we did not forget our mission - the sole reason we existed on earth - to race in such a way that Nobody Beats Us!

27

"I HAVE NO WORDS. MY VOICE IS IN MY SWORD"
MACBETH. SHAKESPEARE
8:30 A.M., SUNDAY, JULY 1, 1984

IN A METALLIC, MEGAPHONE VOICE, THE OFFICIAL SAID, "To the starting line, please."

The time of judgment had arrived: Olympic trials. Double sculls. The finals.

We paddled to the line, quiet and alone, feeling the stiff headwind that blew directly up the course. A headwind was good for us. The race would be longer, thereby giving us more time to crush our opponents. If we had been greeted by a tailwind, I would have thought of some equally good reason why it was to our advantage.

Our warm-up had been ruined a few minutes before when the wake from a referee's launch swamped our double. Perhaps they were allies of Harry, I thought, as we bailed out the water, using our socks as sponges. I kept thinking of something the great Norwegian sculler, Alf Hansen, had told me, "Warming up is important and all, but it sure seems like a waste of time."

I knew exactly what he meant. For this race I didn't require a warm-up. I'd been warming-up for weeks, a lifetime.

Some races are all business. Other races, like this one, are personal.

I tucked the back of my red short-sleeve LIFA shirt into my rowing shorts. This shirt was my armor - I wore this same shirt during almost every practice in Ithaca. I had raced in it at the single trials. This was my power shirt. Red. When push comes to shove, I always wear red - the color of power.

I was a little nervous. Not frightened nervous, just anxious nervous. Ready to kick-ass nervous. Power nervous. Hold tight, my friend, this is going to be a wild ride. This is our private Olympics. This is personal.

As we backed into the stake boat, I looked long and hard over my right shoulder for any debris in our lane. Okay, our lane was clear. I rowed a few half-strokes to align our boat down the course. Okay, we were straight. Then I brought my oar handles together and closed my eyes for a moment. Okay, this is it. I took three deep breaths. I sucked down the nervousness with the first breath. I cast away any doubts with the second. I moved into shadow-racing consciousness on the third. Then I listened for the starting commands.

A few moments later, Charlie Altekruse, in the next lane over, turned to us and said, "Good luck, guys."

Neither Paul nor I responded in any way. We didn't glare at him, or laugh at the absurd timing of his statement. Our silence was the first authentic example of cool we had shown since we arrived in Princeton. I wanted to say, 'You'll need more than luck this time, Charlie,' but I said nothing. Paul said nothing. We kept our eyes locked on the starter's white flag.

Our shadow-racing consciousness had taken over. We had practiced sitting in this exact place, poised and ready, a hundred times, and we knew precisely what to do. No distractions broke through our barrier. Every heartbeat had been unalterably preset.

Charlie tried again. "Good luck, guys," he said, a little louder, as if we might not have heard him the first time. Was he trying to psyche us out, or was he sincere? It didn't matter. My sister, *The Distracter*, had strengthened our concentration with tougher challenges than this. She would be proud.

The starter called our position: "Lane six, prêt?"

No reply needed. Rev it up, Paul, high and hard. Here we go.

"Etes" AD- "Vous" -I- "Prêt"" -OS. "Partez."

We bolted off the line in complete control of our rocket. Dan was right - this boat was a rocket ship. We burned off a little excess energy in the first minute, rowing at 42 strokes a minute for the first ten, nice and high, and then 39 for the next ten. We shifted to a 36 after 20 strokes, and began to lengthen out - nice, long, crushing strokes.

Our boat wobbled for a stroke after the second shift, but then steadied. Be careful, Paul. Be strong, hang onto the finish. That will keep our boat steady in this rough water.

We have the rating we want, now shift into overdrive.

Paul and I signed our name to every stroke. We had our cherished white-hot concentration. We kept our eyes riveted to ourselves, to our ship. My eyes were on his back; Paul's eyes were on the stern. Our double was all that mattered - making our boat fly down the course. Our only challenge was to row as fast as possible. The rest of them? They were back in Lucerne or New York or Hanover.

Five hundred meters.

A hundred people were following the race on bicycles, riding along the path next to the shore. They were yelling something - I couldn't understand a word of it. I glanced across the course and saw that we were in second place. That was okay - don't freak out - we'd shadow raced this scenario a hundred times. But wait a second. Both the Love Boat and Tiff and Dietz were a length behind us. Who the hell was that ahead of us? The lead double was Casey Baker and Dan Brisson.

Baker and Brisson. They won't last, I thought, as we moved past the sloping rock at 750 meters. This was a good place to crank a huge ten-stroke piece.

"Ten for the Easties," I said to Paul.

Yes, with power. Our boat responded. I could sense the speed increase. The Easties knew when to take a power ten. Just when everyone else was settling in, as though the race were a marathon, the Easties always uncorked a blistering ten-stroke spurt. We had watched a tape of them winning the '83 Worlds. We had learned our lesson.

We rowed down Baker and Brisson as we went past the small sign on the shoreline - 1000 meters.

Halfway home for us. Halfway to Hell for them. Have a nice trip. Good luck training for another four years, Charlie. I hope you enjoy the scenery.

Past each buoy. Past the bikes on the path. Past caring about anything, except putting a length between us and them. Come on, Paul, I thought, let's get a length.

"Ten for quicker hands."

Fifteen hundred meters.

Crank on the oars. Fire down the legs. I don't give a damn about the Olympics. Once, just once, I want to see Charlie's head twist around, looking for us. This is personal.

Let's show those guys some endurance. How many blistering, five-minute pieces had our opponents rowed in the last two weeks? How many times, like Paul and me, had they had their asses handed to them by a really fast light-weight straight-four? Not very many by the look of their puddles. Hurts to lose, doesn't it? Hurts like hell. I'd had my turn.

Seventeen hundred and fifty meters.

Pain? Yes, of course. Racing without pain is not racing. But the pleasure of being ahead outweighed the pain a million times over. To hell with the pain. What's six minutes of pain compared to the pain they're going to feel for the next six months or six decades. You never forget your wins or your losses in this sport. YOU NEVER FORGET.

Into the last 20 strokes, we were solid. We held nothing back. The pain was our reward. If it hurt us, it hurts them more. We had the lead, and nothing would stop us. Ten for us. We were the ones. We knew it, but Harry didn't. Make sure he never forgets this moment. Yes, make him remember.

Drive away the puddles, one more inch. Paul looked up, saw our lead, and yelled, "YEAH!"

No. No yelling. Not until we are across the line.

Yes, I feel it too. I feel the intoxicating mix of anger and adrenalin and pleasure at being ahead. I feel that sweet juice beginning to leak out every pore.

"Nobody Beats Us!" I shouted.

The last ten, the hardest strokes of all - make them our best.

The finish line flag cut through the air.

Then the flag stayed pinned to the ground. Even after we shouted our joy and paddled a few strokes and screamed our unbridled happiness, the flag stayed pinned to the ground.

The flag would not come up again until the second place finisher had crossed the finish line.

28

SUNDAY BLOODY SUNDAY
SUNDAY, JULY 1, CONTINUED

SIX SECONDS.

Stop right now and count six seconds. Six seconds is a long winning margin in the sport of rowing. Long enough to paddle a few strokes, to thank Paul for being Paul. We are partners, Paul and I. Partners, plain and simple.

Six seconds. Long enough to close my eyes and remember every beautiful dawn I had the pleasure of seeing while sculling along the quiet waterways of Newport Harbor. Those countless miles had brought me here.

We defeated Tiff and Dietz by six seconds. Casey Baker and Dan Brisson, who had led at the halfway mark, finished third. The camp's finest men, the Love Boat, blessed with Lucerne racing, coaching, money, and equipment, finished fourth. I was glad for Casey Baker. We had rowed together in a quadruple scull at the '77 World Championships, my first year of sculling. Casey was a good man.

Paul and I rewarded ourselves with the longest cool-down in the history of the sport. We didn't talk or shout, at least not after the first minute or two. We paddled at medium pressure, stretching out, thinking of nothing, enjoying a quiet Sunday morning on the lake, two friends on an easy row.

We had done it. It worked. No worries. Clean and quick. It happened so fast. Six seconds. Six seconds is a big, healthy margin. Mike Livingston had been right.

While Paul and I paddled, my old friend Dan Louis launched his quad with Tiff, Charlie, and Joe Bouscaren. Quite a strange line-up, I thought, as they rowed past. I wanted Dan's quad to win, for his sake and for Tiff. But with only a hurried row to the starting line as their sole practice, and with three of the four scullers having already rowed one race, I didn't expect too much.

As Paul and I completed our cool-down, I was reminded of how small the sport of sculling is in the United States. A grand total of three quadruple sculls passed us on the way to the starting line. Three entrants - a feeble number of boats considering that this was the ultimate sculling challenge in which everyone was invited to participate.

As we returned to the dock, the man who greeted us wore a pair of faded jeans and a flannel shirt with the sleeves rolled up, strokewatch around his neck - Tony Johnson. Along with Fin Meislahn, we had a fine reunion. I felt incredibly good, having made them so happy. Their safe haven in the summer storm, and their coaching, had been invaluable.

At the weigh-in station, we balanced our boat on the digital scale. Soaking wet, and with two lead-filled socks, our boat weighted 58 pounds, well over the 57.32 pound minimum.

As we walked the boat toward Tony's trailer, I heard the public address announcer saying the quad race was now approaching the halfway mark. We quickly put our boat on the trailer and turned to watch the final minutes of the race. The quads were close, but not overlapping. One boat was clearly ahead, Bracken's quad, no doubt. After their triumph in Lucerne, I had picked Bracken's quad to win without breaking a sweat.

I made a slight error in that calculation. Four of the scullers in the race had a special fire brewing. These four men were hungry and inspired, and perhaps they had acquired a new confidence after watching our race.

Bracken's quad was not leading, nor was Dan's quad. As they passed directly in front of us, I stared in complete shock. The first place quad, leading by three seconds, was manned by Curtis Fleming, Bruce Beall, Ridgely Johnson, and Gregg Montesi.

Ten strokes later they crossed the finish line in first place.

The instant Curtis's boat crossed the line, I looked toward Harry Parker and Chris Allsopp standing on the shore in front of me. Harry let out a soft cry and seemed to cave in. Only Allsopp's support prevented him from falling. The two coaches embraced, consoling each other without words. I looked away and watched Bracken's quad as they trudged the final few strokes. Those last strokes, when the first place boat has already crossed the line, bring forth a pain straight from hell. I knew from experience.

Six beloved sons, Charlie, Joe, Bracken, Colgan, Purdy, and Frackleton, had died in front of Harry this morning. His dreams of greater glory were over. They had perished before his eyes. Seeing Harry, grey and bent under the pressure of his losses, took the winning smile off my face for a time. Rowing is serious business for a few men, and certainly Harry Parker approached his coaching duties with an intensity and seriousness that few men could match.

An hour later the new Olympic sculling squad held an impromptu team meeting. We stood on the grassy embankment next to the lake, ignoring the oarsmen outside of our circle, smiling like giddy children at the gates of Disneyland. I was ecstatic that Curtis's quad had won. The next few weeks would be easier, I knew, having Curtis and his teammates around as opposed to the guys from Harry's boat.

At first we talked of possible training sites leading into the Olympics and then of the best equipment for us to use. Finally we talked about coaches.

Naturally, I didn't want Harry to remain as the sculling coach, and I expected the other scullers to agree. He had been hired by the Men's Olympic Rowing Committee, and we lacked the authority to fire him. But since both his boats had failed to win the trials, his credibility had been reduced to nothing. We could strongly recommend that he retire, which was exactly the option I offered. A few minutes into our meeting, Harry sent word, via messenger, that he was volunteering to quit.

"Well, that makes things easier," I said, after an appropriate pause.

"Let's talk before we make any decisions," Curtis replied. His motion was immediately seconded by my own partner, and to my surprise, almost everyone wanted Harry to remain as coach. Perhaps Harry's offer to quit had drawn their sympathy, but I still wanted no part of him. My memory of the summer's tribulations extended far beyond the previous hour.

"We should get rid of Harry," I said. "He's on a losing streak, and we can do better. We can get Mike Livingston to be our coach." Curtis and the other scullers had no interest in being coached by Mike Livingston. They didn't know Mike's genius, and his incredible ability to describe the champion's path. Too bad.

Tony Johnson was suggested, but he was already committed to ABC-TV, as a technical assistant for the rowing events at the '84 Olympics.

"Harry is a terrible selector," Curtis said, "but that's over now, and we need him. He'll get the most out of each guy."

"I can't believe what you're saying," I said. "He didn't even invite you to his camp. That should say what he thinks of you."

Only Gregg Montesi, the quiet Navy man, said he wanted no part of Harry. Against my wishes, Harry was retained as the Olympic sculling coach.

Suddenly Charlie Altekruse pulled me aside and said, "I want to be the spare. I'm your best choice. Let's put the past behind us and start fresh. Okay?"

I thought he was joking, and when I relayed his message to Paul and the other scullers, we all laughed.

The spare position is like being vice president. Usually the spare does nothing, except secretly pray that one of the other scullers becomes ill or injured. To some extent the spare sculler enjoys the best of the Olympic world. He is outfitted and feted like a regular competitor. But when race day arrives, he becomes an invisible man. His ghost hovers around the perimeter of the group, carrying oars if needed, smiling and wishing everyone good luck. Then he watches the race from the sidelines.

Usually Coach Harry would have chosen the spare, but for some undetermined reason, perhaps motivated by Charlie's plea, the spare topic was placed on the agenda. I thought perhaps Mike Totta had been promised the spare position back in our Rockywold-Squam Lake days. But here in Princeton, far removed from Squam Lake, Totta's name was never mentioned. We made a quick decision: Tiff was our unanimous choice as spare. He was fun, everyone liked him, and he was an excellent sculler. No doubt Harry would agree with our choice.

At the beginning of Harry's camp, I had remarked to Chris Allsopp that only Biggy, Harry, and he were guaranteed a spot on the Olympic team. In retrospect, I had spoken too soon. Chris was no longer wanted as the assistant sculling coach. His Olympic summer was over, and with great relief, Chris prepared to leave the children of rowing and return to his wife and infant daughter.

Another task, new to the rowing scene, awaited Paul and the members of Curtis's boat. In a ceremonial manner, with many doctors and lab technicians watching, each rower urinated into plastic containers. Tiff and I had performed this strange ritual after the single trials, so no further urine was needed from us.

I was fairly confident that this procedure was a waste of time, although I welcomed the test, to keep everyone honest. As far as I knew, no U.S. scullers bothered with steroids. Aside from being illegal, steroids had the nasty side effect of turning a man's reproductive mechanism to wood. In addition, I knew many weight lifters who popped steroids like M&Ms, and they all exhibited one unifying trait: steroids added to their aggressive personalities. I already had plenty of aggression. One more ounce and I wouldn't survive until the Olympics.

One final pleasure waited to be enjoyed this day. I walked out of the field house where the drug tests were being conducted and over to a familiar box. The first time I had stood in front of this box was in 1974, after I raced in the pair-with coxswain trials. I was eliminated in the repêchage.

I had stood here many times throughout the years, 1975, 1977, 1978, 1979, 1980, 1981, 1982, 1983. Most recently, I had stood here in May 1984, after the single trials, when the news I had to relay had not been good. Times had changed. Now I could enjoy the sweetest part of this whole madness. I phoned home. I told my family and friends that Paul and I had won.

29

CROSS COUNTRY QUARREL
SUNDAY, JULY 1, CONCLUDED

LATE IN THE AFTERNOON, PAUL AND I ARRIVED AT NEWARK International Airport, World Airways terminal.

"Keep out of trouble," I said, as I grabbed my bags.

"You too," he said, "and I'll see you in a few days."

As I waved goodbye, I thought to myself, I'm making a big mistake letting Paul out of my sight. This was my last chance, however, to spend a few days apart from him before our final push to the Olympics. I figured I had earned a break. Too much togetherness, in any relationship, is not healthy.

At World's check-in counter, I unfolded the LA-Newark-LA ticket I had purchased in April. Over the past three months, this skinny lifeless shred of paper had tempted me a hundred times with the promise of a quick escape. Finally, I could succumb to the urge.

Seven hours later my girlfriend, Pam Cruz, picked me up at Los Angeles International Airport. She was all hugs and kisses and, as always, she looked beautiful, lean, elegant. She was tall and blond. Her bright green-grey eyes pierced like diamonds. Pam was a champion swimmer of Olympic caliber.

Pam Cruz. She had an undying belief in my abilities. She was an exceptional woman.

"So, are you here to stay?" Pam asked.

"You better believe it. I'm not going east of the 405 Freeway until after the Olympics."

"Does Paul know?"

"Yeah, he knows."

Paul knew I wanted to stay in southern California. I knew Paul wanted to return to Hanover. Unfortunately, Tony's four-with coxswain entry did not win the trials, and the lightweight straight-four had moved to Philadelphia. Otherwise, we would have returned to Ithaca. Eventually, the lightweights - Toby Wroblicka, John Dervin, John Dunn, and Tony Johnson - won their trials and raced at the Lightweight World Championships, finishing fifth. I'm certain that Paul and I saw these tough, determined men at their fastest, before excessive weight loss cut into their strength.

I preferred training in southern California for a dozen reasons. We needed to become familiar with the hot, dry weather that prevailed at Lake Casitas. The unique lifestyle in California - smog, freeways, In and Out Burgers, everything weird and wild - required more than a few days of acclimation. Also, I had my girlfriend, my Montego, and my family in close proximity.

Something else that Paul and I still required, a daily dose of tough competition, was available in Long Beach but probably not in Hanover. The women's sculling team was training in Long Beach, and their coach, Tom McKibbon, said we would be welcome to race against his crew. McKibbon assured me that the speed of a good women's quad was almost identical to a men's double scull.

Tom McKibbon ought to know. He and his partner, John Van Blom, had been the last American double scull crew to win a gold medal at either the World Championships or the Olympics. They had won by lengths of open water at the 1969 Worlds. Now they were both successful coaches at the Long Beach Rowing Association. How strange that in such an Eastern sport as rowing, the last champions in my event had come from the West Coast, only 22 miles from my home. McKibbon and Van Blom knew a few secrets that I hoped they would impart to us over the next few weeks.

Almost as important, Hanover was overflowing with bad memories. Our independent approach to training life had served us well, and I loathed the idea of exchanging it for the old prison. The more I thought about it, the angrier I became. For hours, one sleepless night, I kept wondering - when does it get easy?

I spent a small fortune on long distance phone calls, attempting to bring Paul to California, but he refused to budge. Hanover was familiar to him, the food was excellent, and best of all, everything was free. The sculling team, Biggy, Curtis's quad, and Tiff, had moved to Hanover, and Paul wanted to stay with his friends and Olympic teammates.

Some of our phone calls turned into heated arguments, and I gradually felt a transformation taking place. Paul and I - two strong-willed men with opposite points of view on an important matter - were becoming adversaries.

Paul and I were a strange combination. We were both blue-collar rowers, persistent, in for the long haul. But if not for rowing, I doubt if we'd spend much time talking at a party. Whenever possible we did not share the same room. Our strength was in our ability to complement each other. We were not a pair of bookends. We were two powerful young men lumped together in a small craft, determined to make the boat fly down the course for six and a half minutes.

Only a few days before, we had conquered the world, and now we were unable to agree on a training site. In an attempt to restore some harmony to our marriage, I decided to return to Hanover.

On the morning of my last day in southern California, Pam and I drove to Lake Casitas for a final, private session on the Olympic course. I had not seen the lake since the 'assault' in January, and I was looking forward to renewing my home court advantage.

At the tiny marina on the lake's northeast shore, Pam and I rented a flat-bottomed, wide-sterned, fishing tub, the only type of rowboat permitted on the lake. The boat was clunky, but the price was right - $7 an hour, which included seat cushions and oars. About noon we ventured onto the lake, tourist style, a young couple on a quiet afternoon outing.

A dozen Olympic construction launches, carrying workmen, buoys, and Styrofoam floats, zipped past us as I rowed out of the protected harbor and into the main lake. Only four and one-half weeks remained until the Opening Ceremonies, with the rowing events beginning the following day. If the speed of the launches was any indication, construction was running behind schedule.

After 20 minutes of easy rowing, I plopped the anchor at the exact middle of the racecourse - lane three, 1000-meter mark - the center of the universe.

I thought about the first time I had ever seen this lake. When Lake Casitas was selected to host the Olympic rowing events, I immediately made a pilgrimage from my home in Newport Beach. I stood on the lake's barren shore, scanning the huge expanse. I snapped a full roll of pictures from that vantage point. Later I glued the pictures together, creating one continuous view of the racecourse. I tacked that master-piece onto my bedroom wall in February of 1981.

Since Olympic-style rowing wasn't permitted on Lake Casitas, U.S. oarsmen would be as unfamiliar with the race-course as the rest of the rowing world. The only exception was one practitioner, a man who had paid homage to the primitive lake by climbing over fences and renting silly tubs.

Only a little wind bothered the surface, yet our boat rocked back and forth. I looked around for a few seconds to find the cause of our rocking. Olympic construction launches, fishing boats, and sightseers were motoring across the lake, each boat generating a separate set of little waves. Paul wasn't too good in rough water, as I recalled. To hell with it, was my next thought. I would worry about wakes and cross-wakes and bumpy water another time. For now I was just another tourist on the lake, enjoying a warm summer afternoon with a good friend.

The next day, Pam drove me to the airport.

Brad Alan Lewis

30

BIGGY'S BIG MESS
9:30 P.M., WEDNESDAY, JULY 4, 1984

ON MY ARRIVAL IN BOSTON, I RENTED A GUTSY LITTLE
Mustang, my way of celebrating the 4th of July, and headed
out of town. About two miles from the airport, I ran into a
major traffic jam. A thousand cars had parked on the Tobin
Bridge, their occupants now sitting on the hoods or roofs,
drinking beer, and screaming their delight as wave after wave
of 4th of July rockets burst overhead. Only one thin lane
remained open for those travelers who did not share the
holiday spirit.

The bright orange sparks cascaded over the blackened
Charles River, making an inspiring sight, but I was too restless
to watch for more than a minute. A long annoying drive
stretched ahead of me, Stoneham, Nashua, Manchester,
Concord, New London, and all points between me and
Hanover, New Hampshire.

I had been without a car during Harry's camp, and to some
extent I attributed my overall failings to a lack of mobility. I
was southern Californian, born and bred, and I needed
constant access to an escape vehicle. The last time in Hanover

I had been at the mercy of others, twice a day, hitchhiking a ride to the boathouse. For a man with a short tolerance for asking favors, this indignity was enough to drive me crazy. I swore that I would never be without my own wheels again.

An hour out of Boston, I felt a strong premonition that Paul had changed his mind about coming to California, and he was, at this very moment, passing me on his way to Boston's Logan airport. I pulled off the road at the next rest stop and called home. My Dad told me that Paul had indeed called only a few hours before, but only to reconfirm that he wasn't moving from Hanover. I had to stop believing those premonitions so readily.

Around one o'clock in the morning, I found the Dartmouth College dorm that housed our rowing team. With school out of session and to accommodate a bigger team, the Chieftain Motel had been retired from Olympic service. I looked for a room assignment list, or for a note from Paul directing me to an empty bed, but I found nothing. Only one room showed a light still burning, and I knocked on the door.

"Come on in," Biggy said. "So you made it. Fantastic. It's pretty hard to find this place, even in the daytime." After talking a few minutes, he posed the question, which I later decided he'd stayed up half the night to ask.

"Say Brad, how would you like to row the single scull in the Olympics?"

"The single? What the hell are you talking about? I see - so that you and Paul can row the double, eh?"

"Yeah, right," Biggy said. "I know deep down you want to race the single, and now I'm giving you the chance. But only if you want it."

"Interesting idea," I said. "Yeah, you're right. I've always wanted to be the single sculler. I think I'll say..."

I was within a breath of saying 'Yes.' The yes-thought had formed in my brain. The yes-word was on my lips.

"I think I'll say... maybe. Tomorrow I'll let you know. It's too late to think clearly."

My last statement to Biggy wasn't true. I knew exactly what I wanted - the single scull. I could train anywhere I wanted. And those few days in southern California had been so sweet. I could be home tomorrow. Yes, I wanted the single, but I wanted a chance to win a gold medal even more.

"By the way," I asked, "Have you talked this over with Paul?"

"Yes, I have," Biggy said. "Paul doesn't care, one way or the other. It's all up to you. But we have to move fast. The entries for the Olympics have to be made by Friday, which gives you only a day to make your decision."

"Okay, but I have another question. Why didn't you ask me over the phone? You could have saved me a lot of money and hassle." For once Biggy didn't have an answer. He just shrugged his shoulders.

Biggy suggested that I take Charlie Altekruse's room, at the end of the hall. Some of Charlie's clothes still hung in the closet, and a few books rested on the desk along with a copy of the school newspaper. This edition happened to feature an interview with Charlie Altekruse, Olympic rower. I glanced at the interview and looked at the clothes and books. Judging from those clues, I decided that Charlie had planned to be away only a short time.

"Don't worry," Biggy said, with a calm, blissful smile. "He won't be back for a while." Biggy hated Charlie.

The next morning I was still undecided - single or double. I wanted the single. I had wanted the single since watching the single finals at the '76 Olympics. I remember so clearly, standing in the cool summer rain, putting myself into the picture. But Mike Livingston's words kept ringing in my ears: "The double is the best event for you."

But if Paul didn't care one way or the other, what did that say about his loyalty to me? He and Biggy were good friends. That must have heightened Paul's indifference toward me. I suppose our hassles about the best training location had soured him on our partnership. I had turned down Tiff's offer. I wonder why he didn't turn down Biggy's? Maybe Paul thought he was doing me a favor by letting me take the single. Ah, the single scull. So tempting.

I opened my door and saw Paul stretching-out in the hallway, in preparation for morning practice. "I guess you've decided to go with the double," he said.

"Okay," I said. "Let's go rowing."

If I decided to abandon the double, I would tell him later. We were still partners, at least for the immediate hour.

Our first task was to find a new boat. After the trials, Paul had literally given away Dan's boat to the women's Olympic double scull team. Dan's boat, made by Van Dusen Boatbuilders of Cambridge, had been virtually perfect, and to find another boat, of similar quality, seemed impossible.

We had plenty of equipment at our disposal. Five boats sat on wooden blocks in a grassy clearing above the Connecticut River. We owned them now, or at least until after the Olympic Games. Like victorious soldiers we picked through the spoils of our little war: a wooden Stampfli, a bright yellow Empacher, two fiberglass Vespolis, and a battleship grey Van Dusen.

"What do you think of the Stampfli?" Paul asked, pointing to the sturdy, Swiss-made boat. A Stampfli was like a fine piece of furniture. I once visited Stampfli's small workshop on Lake Zurich, and watched the old Italian craftsmen creating these floating masterpieces. But unfortunately, Charlie and Joe had used the Stampfli at the trials.

"No," I said. "Bad vibes. Keep looking."

Empachers were the boat of choice by the top European doubles, including the West Germans and Italians. If we rowed the Empacher, however, we gained no advantage over the field. I wanted something special. The Vespolis had a nice hull shape, but they were too heavy for my taste. We needed something extra special - a blazing hot boat.

Only the Van Dusen remained. Mud and leaves caked the Van Dusen's hull. The riggers were spotted with rust. Apparently, this boat had sat through a few summer rainstorms. Charlie and Joe had rowed the Van Dusen only once and then decided it was a piece of junk. Perhaps they were right.

Some Van Dusen's flew down the racecourse, while others sunk at the starting line. Luck of the draw. Was your boat made on a Friday, or even worse, on a Friday before a big regatta, when most of the employees were thinking about their impending race?

Ted Van Dusen's big mistake was in the hiring of rowers to work in his shop. Most of these workers had college educations, fine upbringings, but little experience in using hand tools or mixing resin. Still, on a good day, Van Dusen produced phenomenally light, wonderfully streamlined boats.

I had intimate knowledge of Van Dusen's construction techniques from having worked in his shop in the fall of 1978. A tough season, 1978. My injured right leg was too weak for good rowing. I had absolutely no money, no car, and the weather was turning painfully cold. Then Ted Van Dusen refused to honor a deal we had made, regarding the exchange of my labor for a new boat. Eventually, he sued me and won. I ended up paying him a few hundred dollars.

All debts had long ago been settled, and I had no problem using a boat with his name on it, as long as it was fast. Certainly I couldn't ignore the advantages of this Van Dusen double: she was made in the U.S.A., she was stiff and light and new, the vibes were fine, and the color matched my present state of mind, battleship grey.

Paul and I bolted on the riggers, brushed the snails off the tracks, and went rowing. After ten strokes I understood why the Love Boat had cast it aside. We tipped from side to side without any apparent cause, as if some invisible gremlin was tweaking the hull. No problem. We could fix that by adding a few pounds of lead ballast. We had done the same with Dan's boat, and a similar rocking problem had been greatly reduced.

In the late evening, as I walked back to the dorm after dinner, I suddenly decided that I would forgo the double scull and row the single scull in the Olympic Games. The notion hit me so hard that I began running to Biggy's room. I knocked on Biggy's door and entered without waiting for a reply.

"Biggy, the double is all yours," I said. "Good luck and give 'em hell. I know you guys will do really well."

Biggy sat still a few seconds, and then he said, "I've decided to stay in the single. Sorry if I got your hopes up over nothing. Guess I was a little down when I made that offer."

"You've decided to stay in the single? Well, I'll be damned. Okay, but do me one favor. Don't tell Paul I was going to quit on him. I'd rather he didn't know."

"Sure, I won't say a word."

I walked down the corridor to Paul's room. The door was open, and I saw my partner knitting yet another Christmas present.

"We have much to improve," I said. "Let's go to work."

31

Hanover is Over
July 11, 1984

ROCKING BACK AND FORTH IN THAT CLUNKY ROWBOAT DURING
my last visit to Lake Casitas had given me a slightly new
perspective. On flat water, I knew we were fast, but we had
some bumpy water ahead of us at the Olympic racecourse.

To battle on Lake Casitas, with its rolling, cross-waked,
uneven water, I suggested to Paul that we race at a lower
rating, 33 or 34 strokes a minute, rather than our usual race
rating of 35 or 36. We could be a little more conservative in
our movements at the lower rating, spend a little more time
gliding between strokes, and not be quite as vulnerable to the
rough water. The trick would be in taking down the rating
without sacrificing boat speed. I knew of only one solution to
that problem - increase our brute strength so that we could
add more power to each stroke.

The ultimate power-monster was Pertti Karppinen, twice
Olympic champion, who raced his single scull at the
amazingly low rating of 28 strokes a minute. His huge reach
and awesome power kept his boat moving faster at that low

rating than scullers who rowed at 35 strokes a minute. In hopes of imitating Pertti, Paul and I spent two hours in Dartmouth's weight room every afternoon, lifting hard and heavy, as though we had months to prepare for the Games rather than a few weeks.

We practiced one exercise with extra intensity, wrist curls. Here's a quick lesson in my favorite weight room drill: with your forearms resting on a flat bench, hang your wrists, palms up, over the edge, while holding a standard, 45-pound lifting bar. Let the bar roll down your fingers until it almost drops from your grasp. Then curl the bar back into the palms of your hands. Don't stop curling until your wrists are above the level of the bench. Then relax your wrists, and let the bar roll down your fingers once again. You've just completed one repetition - nine more to go. And then six more sets of ten. I once saw a weight lifter in Gilliam's Gym wrist curl 225 pounds. Good luck.

In rough water, your grips must be held more tightly than in calm water to prevent the oars from breaking loose if smashed by a wave. A tighter squeeze on the grips, when not supported by adequate forearm strength, can lead to cramped forearms, known in rowing as 'fire paw.' The pain of fire paw is unbelievable, and its effect during a race can be disastrous. A sculler's legs might be fresh and strong, but fire paw prevents that strength from reaching the water and moving the boat.

"We'll row nice, even splits," I told Paul, "plugging away, 34 beats a minute. We'll do our best to stay within a length of the leaders. Then with 250 meters to go, we'll uncork a sprint that will spin their heads."

In Hanover, we practiced two new on-the-water drills, MCP, which stood for Maximum Concentrated Pressure, and Perfect Race.

MCP consisted of rowing one or two 2000-meter pieces, at full tilt power, at an extremely low rating, 20-22 strokes per minute. This drill was a combination of rowing and weight lifting. Inevitably we swore and groaned with each drive, doing our best to tear the riggers off the boat. Rather than succumb to the natural tendency to let our blades exit the water before the finish, we made a special effort to hang onto the water until the last possible millimeter, finishing each stroke with our oar handles up by our chests.

Then we took lots of time up the slide, forced control, priming ourselves for the next explosion. If our stroke meter read higher than 22, the piece would become invalid, and we'd have to start over. This was a radical drill for us - from a strictly muscular point of view, we were able to row harder at 20 strokes a minute than at 34. Later, during the high rating workouts, we tried to incorporate the same brutal power that we'd used when rowing MCP. This was my favorite drill, MCP, and a suitable match for my attitude. I loved rowing MCP.

The second drill, Perfect Race, was a little easier on the body, but harder on the brain. By ourselves, we rowed 2000-meter pieces at half power. Each piece exactly as if we were racing in the Olympics. It was somewhat akin to Shadow Rowing, which we also practiced every day, but different, maybe even better, since we were in our watery element. We practiced Perfect Race dozens of times, focusing on making perfect strokes, with perfect control, always with perfect concentration. Sometimes we sprinted at the end of the race, sometimes we threw in a sprint halfway down the course. Sometimes, after all the other boats had gone in for the evening, we rowed for long stretches with eyes closed, imagining that we were at the Olympics, at this exact place on the racecourse, ten strokes to go, ahead. We became quite proficient at blocking out the rest of the world and locking into each other.

Our competition in Hanover came from an unexpected source: the U. S. men's Olympic eight-oared crew.

The eight had recently returned from a ten-week European racing tour, where they defeated all opponents, including the East Germans and Soviets. The eight's only loss was to the Canadian crew on the first day of the Lucerne International Regatta. With such dominating results, the U.S. eight, coach and crew, were expecting to win the gold at the Olympics.

In Hanover, the coach of the eight, Kris Korzenowski, divided his boat into two four-with's, to give his men more competition than if they simply rowed together. With Kris's permission, Paul and I placed ourselves between these speedy four-with's and raced like madmen.

I had a special reason for wanting to win against at least one of the two four-with's: the boat stroked by Bruce Ibbetson. 'Golden Boy' was his nickname back when we both rowed on the U.C. Irvine crew. Throughout my rowing career, Bruce played the invaluable role of my ultra-antagonist. From our first meeting in 1973, we began to build a hostile relationship. I was a lowly freshman oarsman at U.C. Irvine, while Bruce, a year ahead of me, was already starting to shine. Blond hair, strong and powerful, incredibly fit and a fierce competitor, he seemed to win every challenge.

Some of our fiercest battles took place in the pitch black of an early morning workout, running around Balboa Island, streetlights showing the way, shoulder to shoulder, 400 yards ahead of the next runner, neither of us speaking a word for miles on end. The first man back to the boathouse would be champion for the day. More than anything, we both wanted to be that man. For 11 years we fought each other, hard, long, and mercilessly. Occasionally, we wasted our energies by fighting with words.

I didn't know it at the time, but our ongoing feud was providing me with the necessary spark I needed to reach the highest level of my ability. These last few years, during the winter months, Bruce trained in a single scull. The pain I endured to finish ahead of him in those workouts was beyond belief. And many times I didn't finish ahead. When I lost to Bruce, the rest of the day would be hell. Ruined. Utterly ruined.

I'm certain that I would not have made it to Hanover without Bruce Ibbetson pushing me to the edge of my ability.

In Hanover, Bruce and I found ourselves battling one last time. He was the stroke of the Olympic eight-oared crew, the most prestigious position on the sweep team and a job for which he was well suited. We growled at each other on occasion. I once overheard Bruce telling another oarsman that he was certain Paul and I had somehow cheated to win the trials. But mostly we kept our mutual animosity confined to the racecourse.

Bruce's domain, sweep rowing, was wholly different from sculling. He rowed with one oar instead of two, a quicker stroke. Endurance and strategy were less important than lopsided, heavy-handed strength. By necessity, sweep oarsmen always rowed in the company of at least one of their mates. Off the water, they traveled in packs.

Few successful sweep oarsmen made the switch to sculling. From a distance, sculling looked remarkably easy, but sweep-to-sculling converts soon found out the truth. A long apprenticeship, during which the converts were regularly beaten by wimpy scullers, was needed before their ample sweep-muscle could be put to good use.

Scullers, who never switched to sweep rowing, were more like bowlers. We came in all shapes and sizes; we usually bought our own equipment; we dressed funny; we acted strange. A good sculler cherished balance, control, technique, and strategy over brute force. Thankfully, both sculling and sweep rowing were represented in sufficient numbers at the Olympic Games.

Toward the end of the camp, we competed in a wild, four-boat showdown: two 2000-meter races. The eight-oared shell, Curtis's quad, the straight-four, and a special guest quad of Biggy, Paul, Tiff, and me all converged on the starting line. On Harry's orders, the start was to be slightly staggered, to correct for innate differences in boat speed. If all four crews were of equal ability, we would finish in a four-way tie.

A brief, two-mile warm-up would hardly seem to be sufficient practice for my quad to expect a victory over Curtis's quad. They had logged hundreds of miles, and more importantly, they had pulled off a major rowing coup by winning the Olympic trials.

As we left the dock, Harry volunteered a bold prediction. "Based on the results from the single trials," he said, "you guys should win each piece by about ten lengths."

Tiff and I had a good laugh recounting that statement as we rowed to the starting line. If Harry thought that now, then what was he thinking during the five-week camp we had just endured? Too late to worry about such trivia.

In the first 2000-meter race, we bolted from the start like a scalded cat. Within 20 strokes, we had made up our handicap on the straight-four. When I looked over at about 400 meters in, I expected to see Curtis's quad going stroke-for-stroke with us. Instead I saw a cow munching grass on the river bank.

Curtis's quad was two lengths behind and losing ground. They finished ten or twelve lengths to our rear, a margin soon to be repeated in the next race.

Toward the end of the last race, the eight-oared shell, which had failed to catch our quad on the first race, began climbing up our stern. With less than a minute to go, their coxswain yelled, "We have the quad!"

Tiff responded in maniacal form. "Oh no you haven't, you little bastard!"

Tiff possessed the rare ability to scream at the top of his lungs in the very heat of battle, when I might barely manage a whisper. In the last ten strokes, Tiff screamed three or four more expletives at the coxswain, the whole time bending his oars with frightening torque. Thanks to Tiff's cheerleading and his hard rowing, we managed to stay ahead, right through the finish line. Good for us, and especially good for Tiff, Paul, and me. We knew all along that we could move the damn quad.

Hanover, part II, had turned out well. Despite my reservations, once again Paul had been right in his choice of training site.

The last few days, however, turned up one final disagreement. I wanted to compete in a final tune-up race, the U.S. National Rowing Championships, in Los Gatos, California. Paul and I had raced only one regatta, the Olympic trials, in almost a year, and I was certain we needed another regatta to check for any weaknesses in our racing ability.

Paul said no. According to him, our speed was fine, and equally important, he didn't want to miss Sunday's extravaganza - the long awaited, the legendary, the Olympic outfitting. I had little interest in the outfitting. I had seen that movie in 1980, and I wasn't all that interested in another viewing. That's not quite true: I looking forward to getting a new pair of Levi 501 jeans, 35-inch waist, 36-inch length.

Button fly, baby, button fly.

Paul and I struck an unusual compromise. On Friday, I departed for the Nationals, where I would race in the elite single the following day. Paul would leave Hanover with the rest of the squad on Saturday. We would meet in Los Angeles on Sunday, to be outfitted together.

32

THE GURU'S FINAL BLESSING
SUNDAY, JULY 14, 1984

I ARRIVED IN LOS GATOS, AN HOUR'S DRIVE SOUTH OF SAN Francisco, at about 3:30 in the morning, and drove straight to the racecourse. In the lakeside parking lot, I crawled into the back seat of my rented Lincoln Town Car, a great American luxury car and a snug little camper.

I had barely been able to keep my eyes open during the drive from San Francisco, but now, as so often happened, I could scarcely close them. Finally, towards dawn, I slept for an hour, until a blaring loudspeaker snapped me to attention: "Intermediate four-with coxswain, heat number one, please launch your boats."

A few minutes later I found my father. He was standing next to a pick-up truck. Tied to the roof was my single scull. My father, with the help of his friend, Eddie Halpin, had driven ten hours from Corona del Mar to provide me the opportunity to win my first national championship.

Every successful athlete has someone to help him through the big and little hassles. In my case I had two people, my mother and father. They had supported my rowing obsession for a dozen years by giving me a quiet place to live, good food, and every conceivable manner of emotional support. Only with their help was I able to escape the reality of the rent-paying world in favor of the artificial world of rowing. Through the good and bad times, my parents maintained an unwavering belief in me.

My dad had brought me a couple of oranges, but I had no time for breakfast. My race was to begin in 20 minutes. This challenge was unusual. I had not rowed a single scull in months. I had not slept the night before. I was coming off two weeks of tough training, not to mention jet lag, chancy rigging, and a bad lane. If nothing else, I was too tired to be nervous.

I raced a decent piece, strong and aggressive the whole distance. Unfortunately, I didn't win. I finished second to Pat Walters, an excellent sculler from Canada and a friend of mine. In a real surprise, however, I was awarded the gold medal, by virtue of having been the first American to cross the finish line.

A better prize was yet to come. Waiting in the grandstands was Mike Livingston. After the race, Mike and I walked away from the crowd to a rocky embankment shaded by eucalyptus trees.

"How does it feel to be the national champion?" he asked.

"I'm not too excited because I finished second to Pat," I said, "but I'll take it anyway."

"Listen, Brad, you should be excited," Mike said. "To be a national champion is a great accomplishment. If nothing else, you're the only U.S. Olympian to find your way here. Believe me, it's not a coincidence. You fought well on the racecourse. You're a good fighter."

"My teammates are more interested in getting the right shoe size at tomorrow's outfitting," I said.

"How are things going with Paul?"

"Not too well," I said. "We've had a few differences since the trials. Our training is going okay. We're lifting weights and shadow rowing. I think we're rowing fast. The problem is our mental togetherness. It's great on the water, but off the water, it's zero. After the trials we lost that sense of total cooperation. We're damn different as people. He's a good guy - I like him - but he can be stubborn as hell. I wish the Olympic finals were tomorrow so I could be done with this mess."

Mike thought for a few moments. "For the next two weeks," he said, "I want you to change your attitude toward Paul. Like I said months ago, you must row as if your life depends on it. Apply that rule to your new challenge. This friction between you and Paul is working against your goal. And don't think that you can't be pretty stubborn yourself. Now listen - be his friend for two weeks. Treat him like a brother. Keep him happy. Everything you've told me about your training is excellent. You've completed 95 percent of the work. To earn the last 5 percent, you must be in total sync with Paul, like two connected warriors. Don't forget, Brad, you no longer battle alone."

"What the hell," I said. "Okay, I'll treat him right. I can do anything for two weeks. How about you? I'd really like your help during the Games."

"No, I don't think so. You don't need me, Brad. It's only by seizing full responsibility for your rowing that you have reached the Games. The only person with whom you can share the responsibility is Paul. No me, not Harry, just Paul.

"Arlynna and I are going to the Sierras for a few days, and then to the Bay area. After a week we're returning to Hawaii. I might see you again before the Games."

Later in the afternoon, I flew from San Francisco to Los Angeles with Pam, who had watched me race at Los Gatos. While waiting at LAX to catch a commuter plane to Orange County Airport, we experienced the oddest coincidence. From our obscure terminal, looking through a maze of corridors, I suddenly recognized Tiff, Paul, and Biggy as they disembarked from their plane. They could not see me, but I clearly saw them, a foot taller than the crowd. Perhaps this sighting was another important premonition.

"Do you want to go visit with them?" Pam asked.

"I think I'll hold off," I said. "Mike's right. I have to change my attitude toward Paul, and I want to start with our next meeting. I'd best ration my supply of niceness very carefully."

To hell with premonitions.

After the next day's outfitting, during which I received enough clothes to last well into the next decade, the whole U.S. Olympic rowing team, 55 athletes, plus another 50 coaches, managers, and assorted hangers-on, flew to San Francisco and then took a bus to Berkeley for the final training session.

During our two-week stay in Berkeley, I did my best to be Paul's best friend, his number one fan. When he caught a cold, I brought him a quart of fresh squeezed orange juice and a gallon of spring water. When he felt blue, I cheered him up by hanging an inflatable shark from the ceiling of his dorm room. Mike had been right. Things were starting to get better. I didn't share my soul's secrets with Paul, but then again, I didn't do that with anyone.

Over the summer our mascot had become the shark. The particular species didn't matter - mako, tiger, great white. Paul and I were plain, generic, hungry sharks. A small rubber shark had resided on the starboard-bow rigger of our boat during the Olympic trials, and afterward, we taped it to our new double.

The inspiration for this mascot went back a little further. Once, after a particularly nasty workout, Bruce Ibbetson had screamed at me, "Lewis, you always hang back, cruising along like a jerk, until you see an opening. Then you row like a maniac. You're nothing but a shark."

I liked the nickname - or at least I preferred it to his other nicknames for me.

Paul and I continued our heavy weight lifting and tough on-the-water sessions, lining up against the women's eight, the men's four-with coxswain, the straight-four, Tiff and Biggy in a double scull - any crew that would race us. The Tiff-Biggy double proved to be very fast and very determined. On the dozen or so pieces where we battled, Paul and I had to draw on every ounce of energy and every morsel of skill to defeat them. If we didn't, Tiff and Biggy won.

We also continued our shadow rowing. By necessity, Paul and I performed this last drill in front of the whole team. We endured a few mocking laughs from the sweep oarsmen. Keep laughing, I thought. The more distractions, the better for strengthening our concentration. Nothing really mattered by this time - we were so far into our regimen, we didn't care what anyone thought of us.

One week before the Games, Paul and I told Kris Korzenowski that we were initiating a special Norwegian pre-race training regimen, known as 'Supercomp.' I had learned Supercomp during a self-funded, ten-week rowing and racing tour in Sweden during the spring of 1981.

Supercomp consisted of three days of maximum effort sprint workouts, such as four times 1000 meters, six times 500 meters. All six workouts had to be rowed at the highest possible ratings, and all to complete exhaustion. This depletion phase would be followed by a series of easy workouts, leading into the Games.

Korzenowski, the only U.S. Olympic coach familiar with Supercomp, was not in favor of our plan. The Olympics were too soon, he insisted, to allow us enough time to fully recover. I disagreed. We had two full weeks until the Olympic finals. By then we would be in perfect phase.

I clearly remember Korzenowski's final words as we rowed away from the dock for our first Supercomp workout: "If you do Supercomp," he said, "it will be the final nail in your coffin."

33

ALEXI LEADS THE WAY
WEDNESDAY, JULY 25, 1984

OH-LIMP-PEAKS. THREE TINY SYLLABLES THAT CONJURED UP
wondrous images of free haircuts from Vidal Sasson, a red-
white-and-denim wardrobe courtesy of Levi Strauss, and free
trips to Disneyland. I wanted only one thing, a chance to
fulfill a dream that had worn a groove in my brain.

We arrived at the Santa Barbara Olympic Village, on
Wednesday afternoon, three days before the Opening
Ceremonies. U.C. Santa Barbara was chosen as the site of our
Village, rather than U.S.C. on downtown L.A., since it was so
much closer to Lake Casitas, where we would be competing.

We were eager to unpack and visit the dining hall, but first
we had to be issued our identification badges, complete with
picture and bar code.

I soon discovered that the Olympic motto, "Citius, Altus,
Fortius," (Higher, Swifter, Stronger), had been replaced with a
new motto: 'Security Over All.' Three tall fences completely
encircled the Village. The outer and inner fences were of the
ordinary, chain link variety, but the middle fence packed a
50,000 volt wallop. Two security towers within the compound

were manned 24 hours a day, and a police boat bobbed offshore.

A hundred pint-sized security guards occupied our dorm, one guard in each corner, a few at each window, two at every stairway and emergency exit, and at least a dozen more crowded around the main entrance. The guards had only one thing in mind - trading Olympic pins. Fortunately, they were not armed.

The food at the Village, all first class, included fresh fruit, a salad bar, excellent chicken and vegetable entrees, and endless bottles of Perrier. On Mike's advice, I avoided red meat and dairy products since these foods contained too much animal fat, an unequivocal slow food. I tried to avoid refined sugar, but after a day I succumbed to the free Snickers and M&Ms strategically placed in baskets around the Village.

In the center of the Village, a small tent housed an assortment of video games, all rigged to work for free. Not surprisingly, this tent became the social hub of the Village. I played once or twice, but I preferred the Hell Hole in Hanover. Besides, I wanted to save my competitive energy for the races, and equally important, I didn't want to rub shoulders with my opponents.

I spent a few hours next door, in the makeshift movie theater, watching *Return of the Jedi*, *Romancing the Stone*, and *Risky Business*. The theater was packed during the *Star Wars* trilogy, but most of the time it remained empty. The darkened, vacant theater suited me fine. I was out of the hot sun and the movies threw a distracting bone to my hyperactive mind.

I stayed away from the disco, the sauna, the laundry room, and, after one incident, the communal television room on the first floor of our dorm.

In the middle of my favorite show, *Rockford Files*, a man lit a cigarette. He puffed away, stinking up the whole room and making me uncomfortable.

"That's pretty rude," Fred Borchelt said to me.

Fred, from the eight-oared shell, was the senior member of our Olympic team.

"You're right," I said. "I'll get him to stop."

This is my turf, I thought. I don't want some inconsiderate asshole fouling my lungs.

I walked over to the man and said, "There's no smoking in here."

"Where does it say that?" he asked. He was about 45 or 50 years old, strong looking. Up close, he appeared unusually tough.

"No smoking," I repeated. "You must leave or put out your cigarette."

The currently playing episode of the *Rockford Files* wasn't nearly as interesting as our conversation, and naturally, everyone in the room gave us his or her full attention. The man looked at me as though to say, if I catch you alone, I'm going to kill you. Then he dropped his cigarette to the floor and stomped it out.

I went back to my seat and pretended to watch television, but instead I felt my heart flutter at 160 beats a minutes.

After a few seconds, Fred leaned over and whispered, "Do you know who that is?"

"No," I answered, "I have no idea."

"That's Alberto Demiddi, the great single sculler. He's coaching the Argentine scullers."

"Well, he should learn some manners," I said.

I remembered Demiddi very well, although I had never seen him in person. During my first year of sculling, I had acquired a Super 8 movie of the '72 Olympic single scull finals, a legendary battle between Demiddi and the Russian, Yuri Malishev. In the last few strokes, Malishev passed Demiddi and went on to win the gold medal. I studied that movie until the film disintegrated, trying to memorize the right technique so that I could apply it to my own.

After the Demiddi incident, I preferred to watch television on the second floor of our dorm, in a room frequented only by non-smoking Americans.

A terrible rumor became reality during our early days in Santa Barbara: the Soviets would go ahead with their Olympic boycott.

I hate boycotts. Nothing worthwhile can be accomplished by an Olympic boycott. If you have something to say, I suggest you go to the Games, win a gold medal, and then stand on the platform with your fist raised over your head. Put a black glove on your fist if you really want to make headlines. Tommie Smith and John Carlos, who made that dramatic gesture at the '68 Olympics, almost boycotted the Games. Instead Smith and Carlos competed, won their medals, and made a lasting statement.

Of the six finalists from the 1983 World Rowing Championships, East Germany, Norway, West Germany, Finland, Canada, and the U.S.A., five of the crews would be competing at the '84 Games. I sincerely wanted the Soviets and their allies to compete in Los Angeles, but since that was impossible, I could at least take some comfort in knowing that of all the rowing events, the men's double scull was the least affected by the boycott.

On a half-dozen occasions, Mitch Lewis drove from his West Covina home to Santa Barbara and resumed his role as our healer, motivator, masseur, and trainer. I arranged to use a friend's house in downtown Santa Barbara as our massage headquarters and private clubhouse. The ultra-tight security at the Olympic Village made Mitch's entry too difficult, and besides, I preferred a few hours away from the other rowers. Paul didn't always appreciate my desire to leave our Olympic opulence, but he went along.

Mike Livingston was with us, through his motivational tape. I listened several times a day, seeking constant reinforcement. "Be humble. Row as though your life depends on it. Take complete responsibility for the outcome of the race." I chanted those lines like a mantra.

Two rowing machines were brought to our dorm, especially for our use. The long drive to Lake Casitas made our usual twice daily, on-the-water practices impossible. We were fortunate to have shadow rowing to serve as our second workout. Every afternoon, Paul and I walked into the upstairs television room, where the ergometers were kept, and commandeered the place.

After one particularly grueling shadow session, I felt charged with energy and bravado. I jumped up and wrote on the chalkboard, 'NOBODY BEATS US!' Then I signed my statement, 'U.S. Double Scull.' My message stayed on the chalkboard throughout the Games.

On Saturday morning, Coach Harry stuck his head into my dorm room and said, "The bus leaves in five minutes. Better get moving."

"Okay," I said. "I'm coming right now." Harry had given me a wide berth since the trials, which suited me fine. In regard to the Opening Ceremonies, however, Harry made a special impression on me.

With our first race only 48 hours away, I had planned to skip the Opening Ceremonies. A full day's outing to the

Coliseum and back, I decided, was not the best way to conserve my energy. Coach Harry had a different opinion, and on Friday evening he told me in no uncertain terms, "If you don't go to the Opening Ceremonies, you'll regret it the rest of your life."

Harry was absolutely correct. From the moment we left the Village until we arrived at the Coliseum, we were waved to, yelled at, lauded with banners, and treated like honored guests by several million people. When the U.S. Olympic team marched into the packed stadium, the exhilarating cheers made me icy with adrenalin.

Once inside the stadium, Tiff and I joined forces, taking pictures of each other, using our team-issue, Kodak disc cameras. We stood next to our favorite sports heroes, including Steve Scott, who remembered me from our college days at U.C. Irvine, Edwin Moses, Dwight Stones, and the world's coolest athlete, Carl Lewis. I literally had to stand in line to get a picture standing next to Carl, but it was worth the wait: C. Lewis and B. Lewis, one wearing a pair of ultra-cool sunglasses and a pop top hair do, the other with a goatee and crew cut.

On Sunday morning, Paul and I practiced early, drove home in record time, and ate quickly, in order to be plopped in front of the television for the first Olympic event. I don't recall that event, but I clearly remember the last event of the day, the men's cycling road race. More specifically, I remember Alexi Grewal.

Through daily newspaper accounts of his tribulations, I had become a big fan of Alexi's. He had earned his place on the U.S. Olympic cycling team the hard way, through the trials, as opposed to being selected by the coach. The U.S. Cycling Federation had dropped Alexi from the Olympic team after he tested positive for a banned drug, but the testing was later found to be faulty, and Alexi was reinstated one day before the Games. Alexi was a free thinker, an island unto himself, and he raced like a man possessed.

Twenty kilometers from the finish of the 190-kilometer, five-hour race, Alexi broke away from the pack. He looked good in front, leading the world. But despite our cheers, Alexi tired on the next-to-last hill. The Canadian, Steve Bauer, went past him with only a few kilometers remaining. I thought Alexi was finished, but a special fire must have been brewing in the depths of his soul. With excruciating pain clearly etched on his face, Alexi managed to hang onto Bauer. Somehow he regrouped himself in the next minute, and then, with only a few meters to go, he whipped his bike around Bauer in a mad sprint for the finish line. Barely, by only inches, he won the gold.

The room rang with cheers - he'd done it - but so close. And each time Alexi won on the instant replay, we cheered again.

"Nice effort, Alexi," Paul said, when the room had calmed down.

"Right on," I agreed. "Let's do the same."

34

FAUX DEPART
MONDAY, JULY 30, 1984

ELEVEN COUNTRIES HAD ENTERED THE MEN'S DOUBLE SCULLS
event, two heats, first place finisher to the finals, losers to the
repêchage. Heat number 1, our heat, included Norway and
West Germany. These two teams, the same exact men, had
finished second and third at the '83 World Championships.

Each double scull team that was competing at Lake Casitas
had a history, and Paul and I spent several hours examining
their recent performances, especially at the Lucerne Regatta
and the '83 Worlds. I worried about the Yugoslav double.
One man from that team had won a silver medal at the '80
Olympics. The Canadians, fifth at the '83 Worlds, were faster
than ever. The Italians had the world famous coach, Thor
Nilsen, formerly of Spain. One man from the Finnish double
had won a bronze medal at the '82 Worlds. The Belgian double
had been a top finisher in Lucerne.

The Norwegians were my biggest concern. These two men,
Alf Hansen and Rolf Thorsen, won the '82 World Championships. They finished second at the '83 Worlds. They won
the Pre-Olympic Regatta.

At the '76 Olympics, Alf Hansen, with his brother Frank, won Norway's only Olympic gold medal. Eight years later Alf Hansen was tougher than ever. Rolf Thorsen, Alf's young partner, also possessed that peculiar Nordic toughness. They were stoic and proud, almost frightening in their precision - truly beautiful scullers. I wondered how the hell we were going to beat them.

I doubted if our opponents worried about us, which suited me fine. The less attention Paul and I attracted, the easier our task would be, when the time was right, to blow on by.

The Olympics - yes, they really existed. We were here. The time had arrived to put all our hard training to the test. Time to race. I must have tightened my oarlocks a dozen times before we left the dock, just out of nervousness. On our row to the starting line, I tried to get comfortable in my new racing jersey, sliced underneath the armpits to give me a little more breathing room, but to no avail. I wished I could have worn my red power shirt, a second layer of skin to me, rather than this jersey. The buoys, the other boats on the racecourse, my jersey, everything seemed new and strange and specially designed to be nerve-wracking.

We drew lane six, farthest from the grandstands, with the West Germans in lane five. In almost every race during 1984, I found myself in lane six - quite a strange coincidence. Norway was on the other side of the course in lane one.

Paul and I sat poised, motionless, waiting for the starting command. The referee had polled the lanes, and now he was waiting for one last crew to align themselves. At last he dropped his flag and shouted, "Partez."

Our start was perfect. We had the lead by three feet. Suddenly a harsh clanging bell broke our rhythm. The bell signaled a false start.

"I wonder who jumped?" I asked Paul as we paddled back to the starting line.

A young man walked along the ramp that connected the starting platforms. He carried a red traffic cone, cradled in his arms. The cone was used to identify the crew that had false started.

The young man walked past the Norwegians, the Austrians, and the Mexicans. He kept moving down the line, past the Swiss and the West Germans. Only one crew was left. Yes, the bright red cone was placed directly in front of our lane.

We had false started.

How did we manage that bit of sculling insanity? Later I discovered that in the previous race, a four-with coxswain heat, an official had not called a blatant false start against the British crew. This same official, Martha Ferguson, an American and a friend of mine, no less, had kept a very close eye on our race. She caught us leaving a tiny bit early.

Now we had trouble. If we false started again, we would be instantly disqualified from the Olympics. Time to use caution.

On the restart, Paul and I tiptoed off the line, as though bringing up the rear of a funeral procession. The other boats blasted away in fine form, leaving us to bounce in their wakes.

By the 500-meter mark, the West Germans had a two-length lead. But to my frantic relief, Paul and I had stopped losing ground to them. Crossing the 1000-meter mark, we trailed by only one length of open water, and instead of being in last place, we were in third, behind West Germany and Norway.

We fought a good battle in the next two minutes. We attacked with 'tens.' We brought up the rating. We were flying. I was furious at our false start, and I spent my anger in the best possible way - driving with my legs, bending my oars, encouraging Paul. In the third 500, we passed Norway.

Stop the race. Let me take a picture. To pass Norway, the toughest team, in the toughest segment of the race, was a fantastic accomplishment.

Coming into the last 20 strokes, only the West Germans, a half-length ahead, stood between us and a direct place in the finals. We closed another ten feet on the Germans. From the corner of my eye, I saw the bowman, Andreas Smeltz, looking harried, overworked. Another 100 meters and we would have them.

"Come on," I said. "Ten to catch 'em." On the sixth stroke of our 'ten,' we ran out of racecourse.

The West Germans won by a second.

35

TO FISH OUT
THURSDAY, AUGUST 2, 1984

NOW WE HAD A PROBLEM. THE WEST GERMANS AND THE winners of Heat 2, the Belgium crew, were safely in the finals. Paul and I had to finish first or second in our repêchage, or we would be relegated to the worst possible fate, watching the double scull finals from the shoreline.

Repêchage, or reps, is French for 'to fish out.' In rowing, the word means that you get a second chance to make the finals, or more accurately, a last chance to make the finals. The reps are the stuff of nightmares. If you were to clip a buoy, or drop an oar, or make one tiny mistake, then adios, see you on the shore. If you have an off day or come up against an inspired opponent, then again, adios.

For us, winning the reps was not especially important. Our real goal was to finish no worse than second place, because both the first and second place crews advanced to the finals.

In the interminable three-day stretch between the heats and our repêchage, we practiced a thousand starts, either on the water, or in shadow rowing, or in our dreams, to make sure we had every advantage going into this race.

For a change we drew lane one, with the Yugoslav crew in lane two. Finland, in lane three, was stroked by Reina Karppinen, brother of the legendary single sculler, Pertti Karppinen. Our draw would have been much harder if Norway had been in our rep.

Waiting on the starting line, I shook my arms, trying to get rid of my nervousness, but to no avail. I knew the only solution to ending this nervous discomfort was to get this race over as fast as possible, with no fireworks or close finishes. Maybe we could discourage our opponents by hammering out a two-length lead in the first 1000 meters. No, bad idea. No one at this level of competition discourages very easily, if at all.

On the word, "Partez," we rolled into the first stroke, clean and fast and legal. After 20 strokes, or about 20 - I always lost count around 15 - we shifted to 33 strokes a minute. We were ten feet behind the Yugoslavs coming off our shift and about half a length ahead of the other boats. Then we started to lean on the power.

The racecourse was mirror smooth this morning, calm, unruffled. We were rested and fully prepared to battle the whole 2000 meters. All the nervousness I had been carrying on my shoulders the last few days was now gone, vanished, as if it never existed. I was doing what I was made to do.

At the 500-meter mark, I began dividing the racecourse into fine little pieces, using the rower's common denominator, solitary strokes. Our boat traveled just under ten meters to a stroke, 60 strokes to each 500-meter segment, 240 strokes for 2000 meters. I counted off the strokes with digital precision, as if by carefully tallying them I could shorten the race. We were in perfect qualifying position, dead even with Yugoslavia and a length ahead of the third place boat. The other boats trailed us by three or four lengths of open water, in rowing terminology, 'a curve of the earth.'

A laser surveying tool could not have divided the last 1000 meters more precisely. A quick glance over my left shoulder gave me a textbook full of information - the distance to the finish line, 620 meters, 73 strokes, one minute 57 seconds. The distance to our closest opponents - we had a two-foot lead over the Yugoslavs, now three feet, now back to two feet. The distance to the other boats - I detected no sign of life. The distance to the edge of our lane - we had ten feet on port side, 16 feet on starboard side. My internal calculator spewed out the numbers.

Last 500 meters. Slice the racecourse, dice it, chop it into tiny morsels, divide and conquer. In the last minute, I started counting 'tens.' I rowed two sets of ten, and then I started counting 'fives.' Five strokes, a deep breath, and then another five. One more 'five.' Okay, good job.

One final press with my legs.

In those last few strokes, my ears were tuned to one specific frequency. I was eager to hear the distinctive finish line beep, which signaled that a boat had crossed the line.

In mid-stroke the beep sounded. Yes, finally. I looked over to make sure the beep was for us. Yes, we were across. Then I looked in the other direction, and saw the Yugoslavs crossing the line. A second beep emanated from the judges platform. We finished first, ten feet ahead.

Stop rowing, Paul, and let the momentum carry us along. I put my hand on Paul's shoulder, and said, "Good row, man." This repêchage race was our first international victory.

Racing in the repêchage had actually helped us, or at least that's what I told myself. Seven long days stretched between the heats and the finals, thus the heat winners, West Germany and Belgium, had not raced in a considerable time. I hoped they had grown stale, fat, bored, distracted, waiting impatiently on the sidelines, playing video games in the Village while gorging on peanut M&Ms. Paul and I would be ready for them on the day of the finals.

A major surprise occurred in the other double scull repêchage. Norway, which I had figured to win a medal, finished third in their repêchage, thus failing to make the finals.

Sorry, Alf, time for a new champion to be crowned.

Later in the morning, Curtis's quad finished fourth in their repêchage. Curtis's quad was the only U.S. boat, either men's or women's, not to make the Olympic finals.

Curtis's quad had followed one of the time-honored axioms of U.S. rowing: it's better to peak at the trials, than never to peak at all. They tried their best, which is all that can be asked of any athlete.

36

THE SHINY DISK
SATURDAY, AUGUST 4, 1984

THE WOMEN'S FINALS WERE HELD ON SATURDAY, ONE DAY before the men's finals.

After our practice, Paul and I watched the races while sitting in the shadow of the huge scoreboard next to the finish line. Like almost everyone in the crowd, I soon became bored with the national anthem that kept being repeated as the races progressed.

The Romanian women, husky, powerful, well-fed citizens, won everything, the single, the double, and the quad, along with the pair and the four-with coxswain. Only the eight remained.

In the last event of the day, the U.S. women's eight, coached by Bob Ernst, my old college coach, sprinted to the lead right off the start. Then they barely held off the hard-charging Romanians to win the gold. Excellent. Good for them. The American women had set the precedent. Tomorrow we would have our turn.

As Paul and I walked past the refreshment tent, I saw the coxswain of the Romanian four-with. The bright ribbon around her neck, a wide band of dark pink, a middle band of soft orange, and a third band of turquoise, indicated she was wearing her gold medal. Without hesitation, I walked up to her. I wanted to see the prize.

The Romanian coxswain did not speak English, but she knew exactly what I had asked. She reached into her T-shirt and pulled up the medal - the shiny disk, the great golden carrot, parlayed into a lifetime's security by some athletes, stuffed into a dresser drawer by others.

Paul didn't want to look. "No thanks," he said. "I'll wait until I have my own."

I cradled her medal in my right hand. It had a solid heft, a weighty feel. The medal fit nicely into my palm. I looked into the coxswain's face. She was in pure heaven, the proudest woman in the world at that moment. I looked down at her medal.

On the side facing me was a woman dressed in robes. She looked sturdy, full-breasted. In her right hand, she held aloft an olive branch. In her left hand, she held strands of wheat. Two small horses, harnessed to a nearby chariot, were nibbling at her robes. These words were inscribed on the top portion of the medal: XXIII OLYMPIAD, LOS ANGELES, 1984.

I turned it over: seven men in loincloths carried one man, the victor. He also grasped a few stalks of wheat in his left hand. With his right hand, he pointed to the heavens.

Appearances are easy to describe. The real essence of her gold medal is more difficult to convey. I felt her medal in my hand. I felt the sensations - pure, heartfelt, unadulterated, undiminishable power. For me, this trinket, this hunk of costume jewelry, possessed the power to give me the freedom that I'd been seeking for the last ten million strokes.

"Let's go, Brad," Paul said. "We better hurry or we'll miss the van."

"Nice," I said to the woman. "Very, very nice."

She nodded and slipped the medal underneath her shirt so that only the ribbon showed.

Brad Alan Lewis

37

MITCH'S MAGIC AURA BALANCING
6:13 A.M., SUNDAY, AUGUST 5, 1984

I WOKE UP EARLY AND RUSHED TO THE DINING HALL TO EAT a light breakfast of orange juice, toast with a dash of honey, and half a banana.

My nerves were already on edge so I skipped my usual morning coffee. I sat with no one and I ate quickly, trying my best to ignore the noisy activity around me. Perhaps Paul had been right to stay in his room and skip breakfast. I had left him at the dorm, gathering up T-shirts that he wanted to trade with other oarsmen after our race.

A few minutes later, I hurried to the Village's main entrance to catch the van. Coach Harry sat impatiently at the wheel, wondering why we had conspired to torture him one last time by being late.

Eventually, Paul came trotting down the sidewalk, carrying two duffle bags stuffed with clothes he intended to trade with other rowers at the traditional post-race swap meet. I worried that Paul might strain his muscles lugging them around, but I said nothing. Paul slammed the door, and we were on our way to Lake Casitas.

Mitch was waiting at the racecourse when we arrived. Harry wanted no part of the next act, so he excused himself and walked into the competitors compound.

"Good," Mitch said. "Now, let's get down to business."

Amid the odd stares from passing spectators, Mitch set up his massage table in the parking lot and went to work.

Paul climbed onto the table and stretched out. Mitch gave him a thorough going over, as he had done all week, testing Paul's leg lengths and giving him a full round of chiropractic adjustments.

Lastly, Mitch used his special skill: he balanced Paul's aura. Like myself, Paul was skeptical at first, but having endured one aura balancing session at my urging, he instantly became a convert. After ten minutes of work, Mitch announced that Paul's aura was flawlessly balanced and that he was ready to win.

My turn was next, and Mitch wasted no time in cracking my back at every vertebra, crunching my legs until they were exactly the same length, and then twisting my neck until I felt like an owl.

Lastly, Mitch balanced my aura. Before describing the method, I should note that I lack any scientific findings to verify the legitimacy of the whole, bizarre, aura-balancing madness. But I know it works.

Every person has their own aura, Mitch explained. If their aura can be increased to a maximum level, then that person will be capable of producing his ultimate effort. The common phrases, 'I had a bad day,' or 'I never felt better,' both had their origin in an athlete's aura. Using aura balancing, the 'up' day coincided with the day of the big race - today.

Mitch measured my current aura with a simple strength test. While lying flat on the massage table, I tried to lift my outstretched right arm. At the same time, Mitch, standing just to my right, pressed down on my arm. I could not resist his efforts for more than a second or two, and like always, he clucked his tongue and said my aura couldn't win a game of dominoes in its present state. Then he rapidly massaged a point on my stomach, slightly above my belly button. Again and again he tested my arm strength, followed by more stomach massage.

Every few minutes, he would traverse my whole body with his left hand, always passing a few inches above my skin. I could sense the movements of his hand, even with my eyes closed.

Gradually, almost by magic, my strength increased. Using the same strength test as in the beginning of the balancing, I was now able to resist any amount of his downward pressure. After ten minutes of nonstop work, Mitch was satisfied. My aura was balanced, and like Paul, I was now capable of walking through the fires of hell in order to reach my goal.

As I stood up, a warm, deep flush enveloped my body, and then a solitary thought enveloped my consciousness: We were going to win.

I gave Mitch a big hug, screamed OO-SO at him, exactly as I had done before the single trials. Then I climbed into my familiar cocoon - Walkman and sunglasses.

I listened to Mike's tape as we walked to the boat tent. Then I listened to the Sex Pistol's *Sub-mission* while we put the boat in the water. *Sub-mission*'s deep, tough, relentless beat was exactly the rhythm we needed on this cool, foggy morning.

Brad Alan Lewis

38

ÉTATS-UNIS, PRÊT?
7:50 A.M., SUNDAY, AUGUST 5, CONTINUED

"YOU HAVE 35 MINUTES UNTIL RACE TIME," HARRY SAID.
"Get a good warm-up, get to the starting line on time, and then give 'em hell." His nervous gestures and shifting eyes betrayed the wild anticipation beneath a very thin layer of cool.

"Okay, Harry, see you when it's over."

I tried to think of something clever to say, but without success. I wanted to be away from Harry before his nervousness broke through the barrier I had so carefully constructed that morning.

Paul waved to someone at the head of the dock, and then he said, "Let's do it, Brad."

In unison, we stepped into our double scull. After slipping my feet into the shoes, I gave our mascot, *Sharkie*, a squeeze around the flanks. *Sharkie* responded with a goofy squeal. Harry cringed at the sound, or perhaps he cringed at the thought of relying on luck or mascots or superstition. Paul thought the noise was funny, and it helped break the tension.

"Don't be denied," Harry said in his powerful Zeus-voice, which he saved for these special occasions. This was the Harry I knew - alive with brimstone and fire. I nodded in agreement and forced a smile. But again I said nothing. Over the past three months, we had given each other a lifetime's worth of trouble.

"Ready to shove?" I said. "Ready. Shove."

We pushed off and let our boat glide from the dock. Finally, we were under way. I welcomed the curtain of privacy that descended the second we freed ourselves from the constraints of land.

"Oops, I've got a little problem," Paul said after a few strokes. "My oars are in backwards."

Paul stopped rowing, and frantically began loosening his oarlocks. While Paul switched his oars, I tried to recall his ever having made this rookie mistake. A few seconds later, we rowed toward the starting line.

For the next few minutes, as we paddled easily, I told Paul about the time I saw the famous East German double scull team of Dreifke and Lange at a big regatta in Europe.

"You really had to be there, Paul, it was great. A few yards from the dock, these two giant Easties started yelling at each other, and sure enough, Dreifke had his oars in backwards. Then they laughed like hell. A few minutes later they kicked ass on the best doubles in the world. Don't sweat it, Paul, we'll do the same."

The story about the Easties was true, although it didn't occur at the Olympics. Actually, it happened before a preliminary heat, so the stakes were not nearly as high. The message - that even the best scullers occasionally get their oars mixed up - was still valid, and Paul liked the story.

Our warm-up continued without a problem.

Thirty minutes later we arrived at the starting line and backed into the floating platform. I looked over the competition, all champions, all tough, all certain of victory. Only the finest oarsmen in the world are permitted to assemble at the starting line on the day of the Olympic finals.

Without a doubt, the next few minutes were the most hellishly exciting in my life. Grinding pain and killer fatigue waited just beyond the word 'Partez.' I tried to ignore those prospects and concentrate on the priceless feelings that also waited. I thought about the perfect strokes we would take and about the merciless surge of power we would unleash in the last 500 meters.

I slapped my face two or three times with both hands, as hard as possible. The slapping hurt. It snapped me to attention. My adrenalin started flowing. I learned this slapping trick in the weight room, where we referred to it as 'Getting Fired Up.' Paul had seen me do it before, but the Yugoslavs, sitting in the next lane, stared at me in disbelief. The harsh slapping made me angry - exactly what I wanted. I did my best work when I was angry.

I took a drink of water and handed the bottle to Paul. Then I carefully dried my oar grips with a towel. Lastly, I dried my hands. Paul handed the water bottle back to me, and I poured the last drops over my back. No sense starting off hot and bothered. I stuffed the towel and water bottle into a bag and threw it to the stake boat boy. Not an ounce of extra weight would ride with us.

We had lane six, again on the outside of the racecourse. Other rowers might not like this lane, thinking it was too far from the heat of battle, but I preferred it out here. Today the racecourse, lane six especially, was Sunday morning quiet. A light fog played on the water near the finish line, slowly being chased away by a lazy crosswind.

A huge motorboat carrying the ABC television crew was hovering just to our starboard. On board I saw Dick Erickson and Stan Pocock, both legends in American rowing. At the wheel stood a true rowing champion and one of my heroes, Conn Findlay. He won two Olympic gold medals, in the '56 and '64 Games, rowing the brutal, pair-with coxswain event. Through old rowing magazines and secondhand stories, I had learned that both of his Olympic victories were of the classic, come-from-behind style.

Conn had visited Ithaca this summer and had offered us his own special brand of encouragement, a few subtle words, the slightest nod of reassurance. When I looked toward Conn, he gave us a thumbs-up salute.

In another launch was Tony Johnson, looking very sharp in his ABC-TV windbreaker. I'm sure his old flannel shirt was hidden underneath. At the 1968 Olympics, Tony and his partner, Larry Hough, had led the pair-without coxswain race the whole 2000 meters. The East Germans passed them on the last stroke. Tony and Larry lost by twenty-five hundredths of a second. For eternity, a silver medal was welded to their souls.

The starter lifts his white flag. With his right hand, he grasps the trailing edge and draws the flag taut. Then he polls the crews:

"République Belgique, prêt?" They'll be tough.

"Canada, prêt?" Storm and MacGowan scare me.

"Allemagne, prêt?" Schmelz and Agrikola are the guys to beat.

"Italie, prêt?" No problem.

"Yugoslavie, prêt?" Good scullers.

"Étas-unis, prêt?" Believe it.

I whisper to Paul, "Stay cool off the line. First ten strokes for technique only. Remember: Nobody Beats Us."

The starter drops his flag, and says, "Partez!"

Brad Alan Lewis

39

Nobody Beats Us
8:33 a.m., Sunday, August 5, continued

Partez!

Cool. Careful. Nothing funny. Stay cool.

We are behind. I can tell. We drop back quickly, while the crews in lanes two and three pull ahead. Our rhythm is okay, leg drive strong, rating perfect at 35, no problems, but everyone is moving away. Concentrate. Don't be distracted. We have plenty of time. Just row our race, low rating, strong strokes.

Paul doesn't look around and neither do I. We keep our eyes focused tight and straight. The ABC launch stays even with us, and then falls back. I know Conn and Tony are watching, disappointed.

The world is listening to Curt Gowdy's stroke-by-stroke commentary: "Belgium the leader, Canada number two, and Yugoslavia right now is running third. Italy, in the blue, is running fourth, and Federal Republic of Germany, considered by some the favorite for the gold, is a close fifth."

Curt Gowdy does not mention us. To hell with Curt Gowdy. He doesn't know a thing about rowing or about us.

Paul and I know. We'll crush these guys, but not yet - not too soon. Stay cool.

Five-hundred-meter mark. We have stopped losing ground, and maybe, just barely, we're moving back. Use strength, Paul, long and low, good speed with controlled effort. A bigger surprise is on the horizon. We've prepared for this. Relax and let the shadow rowing take over. We knew our task would be hard. Otherwise it would mean nothing. Be patient, Paul.

Thousand-meter mark, halfway, yes. We moved nicely in the second 500, good job. Only one length between us and third place. Start to move now. Move on them.

"Hands," I say. "Ten to move the hands quicker."

Through 1250 meters, we jump ahead of the West Germans into third place. They spent themselves in the first 1000 meters. I had seen that movie, and I knew it hurt like hell. They won't be back.

We have a bronze medal - an Olympic bronze medal.

Look at us, Olympic medalists, but it's the wrong color. Exchange it for another. We're capable of better. Throw that bronze medal into the lake.

"Let's get 'em!" I yell. Yes, yell for once, not whisper.

Our rating moves from 35 to 36. Nicely done, sharp and crisp, good leg drive, powerful finishes, full reach, quick hands away at the finish. Be strong. MCP, maximum concentrated pressure. No tomorrow, no waiting, nothing beyond the moment. We seek the perfect balance - total abandon on the drive, total control on the recovery.

Last 500. We move past the Yugoslavs into second place, behind Belgium. To hell with the silver medal. I don't want the silver. I want my torture to end. Then I can be free. I will do it here, now, in this moment, with these strokes, with the strength of my body, with the strength of my soul. Dig in.

The pain is so bad that I can't even allow myself to acknowledge it. Good place to die, beautiful place. Make the puddles sing, torque the blades, feel the grips like extensions of our arms, feel the connection between our souls and the speed of the boat. Forget the opponents, only our speed is important. Ignore the outside world, feel the boat respond, the effort is instantly rewarded. Humility, yes. Racing as though our lives depend on it, yes. Now take responsibility for the outcome.

Thirty strokes to go.

"Ten for New Zealand," I say.

The New Zealand eight-oared crew sprinted from last place to first place at the '82 Worlds. In Ithaca we watched that video tape so many times that it runs like a loop inside my head.

The New Zealand crew sat up straighter in the last 500 meters. Now we do the same.

They drove harder with their legs. Now we do the same.

They attacked with lightning precision. Now, Paul, we attack like ravenous sharks.

Twenty strokes. My port oar almost hits a buoy.

"Careful," Paul says.

During the whole race, he says only that solitary word, *careful*.

I almost hit another buoy, but my port oar lifts over and clear. We are veering off course, toward port, heading into lane five. But with Paul's help we straighten out. We'll be okay until the finish, just so we get there first.

But we are running out of racecourse, just like in the heat. Fight like hell, Paul. Let's drive our bow into the lead.

"Ten for NOBODY BEATS US!"

Dig in. Last ten strokes. Everything now, every ounce of

power, all our strength, complete abandon. We cut through the pain. We are poised on the edge of perfection. Yes, we'll take the risk, the big gamble. We commit wholly to the test.

We can do it.

Five strokes. We trail them by a foot. We can do it. The finish line is so close I can taste it.

We can do it.

Four more strokes. Call on the strength that only we possess.

We can do it.

Call on the endurance we earned in Ithaca.

Two more strokes. Call on the intensity that sets us apart from the rest of this whole fucking world.

One last stroke.

We can do it.

The finish line horn beeps. A second later it beeps again.

40

OLYMPIC HEAVEN
SUNDAY, AUGUST 5, CONCLUDED

WE WON.

Belgium next. Yugoslavia third. One and a half seconds separated us from Belgium. The crowd screamed so loud when the official results were flashed on the scoreboard that I can still hear the echoes of those cheers.

For one long moment, heaven existed on earth. Paul and I hugged and shook hands, and then we hugged again.

"We did it, Paul. You and me."

The ABC launch with Conn at the wheel came up to us, and Paul and I shook hands with my hero, and now our peer, Conn Findlay.

After a few minutes, we paddled easily toward the awards dock. I tried to comb my short hair using water from the lake, but it refused to stay put. As soon as we climbed out of the boat, we shook hands with the Belgians and the Yugoslavs. Everyone seemed in good spirits, especially the Yugoslavs.

As we slowly walked up the ramp to the awards platform,

I saw my mother and father, sister Valerie, brother Tracy, cousin-trainer Mitch and his wife Janice, my girlfriend Pam. I saw my training partner Dan Louis. I even saw Steve Reichert, who had asked if I wanted to try sculling way back in 1970.

Paul and I stood in the middle of the platform. I was glad that the platform was level rather than raised in the middle for the gold medal winners. The Belgian and Yugoslav teams had fought well, and they deserved equal respect.

An international rowing delegate walked onto the platform, followed by a young woman carrying a tray. The official walked up to us, nodded solemnly, and then smiled and shook our hands. As my name was called over the public address system, he delicately lifted the medal off the tray and began to extend it towards Paul. I put my hand in front of the official, and motioned him towards me.

My name - my medal.

He understood. The official lifted the ribbon over my head and settled the medal so that it hung evenly on my chest. Then we shook hands again.

As Paul received his medal, I suddenly realized how much bigger he was than I. He seemed huge. Having this man, Paul Enquist, a quiet fisherman from Seattle, as my partner, had been my finest blessing.

He was strong and tough to the very end.

He had put up with my madness all summer long. I am lucky to count him as my friend. Our friendship, like the bond that exists between two brothers, will endure as long we live.

My sister Valerie yelled to me, "Stand up straight when they play the anthem."

I have always enjoyed the national anthem, but never more than this rendition. And thanks to Val I made a special effort to stand up straight. I stood so straight I almost fell over backwards. I didn't cry. I held my hands behind my back, chest out, head held very high.

We had done it. The dream had become reality - sitting in that donut shop in Ithaca, New York, planning, plotting, thinking of ways to make it happen. Then putting those plans into action - five times five minutes. Humble. Six times 500 meters. training and racing as though our lives depended on it. Weight lifting. Shadow rowing. More 500s. MCP, Maximum Concentrated Pressure. Perfect Race. Taking complete responsible for the outcome of the race.

Yes, the dream had become reality - that is an incredible feeling. We triumphed. The sweetest happiness I had ever known - even imagined - emanated from the core of my soul.

Instead of walking directly back to our boat after the national anthem, I made a brief detour. I crossed a narrow section that separated the awards platform from the spectators.

My family was at the front. I hugged my father and mother. For a long moment, I hugged Pam. Tears. Then I handed Valerie the flowers I had been given. Lastly, I hung the medal around my mother's neck.

Paul and I rowed to a quiet part of the lake, to be alone, to relax, to talk about life and love and friendship and passion, of Tony and Conn and Harry and Hanover, and the feeling of being so close to your soul that the recollection - only minutes old - brings on a wave of adrenalin, so you have to talk about something else or drown in the depths. Two men on a quiet Sunday row.

We watched as Biggy finished fourth in the single scull, about two seconds behind third place. As expected, the big Finnish sculler, Pertti Karppinen, won his third straight gold medal. He had a tougher time than many people realize. He trailed the West German, Peter-Michael Kolbe, until the last 20 strokes. Their close battle was almost identical to the race I had seen in Montreal, eight years before, where I watched the single scull finals from the standing-room-only side of the race course.

The U.S. eight, the four-with coxswain, and straight-four all finished second.

When the regatta was over, Paul and I had won the only U.S. men's rowing gold medals at the '84 Games.

Our victory was the first rowing gold for the U.S. men since 1964. It was the first double scull gold for the U.S. since the 1932 Olympics were last in Los Angeles. My dad had been a spectator at those Games, a long, long time ago.

As we rowed back to the dock, Paul asked, "Why did you give your medal to your Mom?"

"I have a lifetime to enjoy the medal," I told him. "I want her to enjoy it now. Besides, the medal isn't important to me. All that matters is that I'm free."

EPILOGUE

THE PUZZLE IS COMPLETE

OVER THE YEARS, EVERY ONE OF MY WORKOUTS CONTRIBUTED a solitary piece to a massive puzzle.

I remember one workout, an afternoon row in Newport Harbor, spring 1977 - the harbor alive with whitecaps. I rowed from Red 8 to the finish line, a three-mile piece into a blistering headwind, just for the hell of it, just to see if I could do it without sinking.

I remember thinking afterwards: that was really great. I'll do it again tomorrow.

As I step back and watch the lines between the pieces fade into oblivion, the puzzle I worked to hard to assemble shows itself to be a self-portrait, Bradley Alan Lewis, or just plain Brad. My rowing career earned me only one lasting thing - myself.

Simple stuff, rowing, and for me the reward is everlasting. I could not have arrived at this place any other way.

Harry greeted us at the dock when Paul and I returned.

I'd never seen him so animated, so happy. All was forgiven. Not forgotten, just forgiven. We shook hands and talked and laughed. Harry showed us the official splits for our race. Under fairly slow conditions, with a cross-head wind and numerous wakes, we had rowed the first three 500-meter pieces in 1:37.45, 1:40.60, 1:40.68. In the last 500, where we sprinted like mad, we rowed 1:38.14, three seconds faster than the Belgian team. Good, confident, almost even split rowing.

Needless to say, I didn't win the Olympic lottery. Mary Lou Retton had the right number for the 1984 drawing. Certainly, my goatee and Marine haircut didn't help my chances of gaining Olympic fame. I looked like a tough, angry young man.

My sense of humor was even less suited for general consumption. I told one interviewer - I believe he was with ABC Radio - that I trained on an exclusive diet of Coors beer, extra-crunchy Cheetos, and Double Stuff Oreos. A rich man is someone who needs nothing, and I was so happy, so content, so totally satisfied with everything I already possessed, that I considered myself to be the richest man on earth. I needed no further reward.

All blisters and wounds soon healed. All debts were soon settled, including reimbursement for the rental of Dan's boat by the U.S. Olympic Committee. All problems evaporated into nothingness. Eventually, my medal became the reclusive resident of Wells Fargo Bank safe deposit box #3636, along with a pair of Levi 501 jeans with gold-plated rivets, a gift from Levi Strauss to all American gold medal winners.

For the first time in years, I felt free to do anything I wanted on the face of the earth. Two days after we won our gold medal, I expressed my freedom by going surfing at 56th Street in Newport Beach, one of a dozen surfers in the water, completely anonymous, exactly the way I wanted it.

Anger. What happened to the anger? Much to my relief,

the anger I had been carrying inside me for so long gradually surrendered its hold on my soul. Once in a while, triggered by some assumed injustice, it comes back for a few days or a week. To be honest, I wish the anger would come back more often, so I could possess the wild energy like in the old days. Mostly I try to live by a new rule: only amateurs stay angry.

Pam and I had a great time on the 'round-the-country tour for Olympic medalists, sponsored by the Southland Corporation. I met dozens of my Olympic heroes while visiting Washington, New York, Florida, and Dallas. I could not imagine a better way to finish my Olympic dream.

At the Olympic tour's final stop in Dallas, I bought a Kaypro computer, and as soon as we arrived home, I began writing this story. My first draft was unreadable. I wrote second, third, and fourth drafts. With each draft, I gradually peeled back the layers, getting rid of the meaningless fluff and nonsense. I sought to capture the spirit of the men, and of the fantastic times we shared. When I began rowing in high school, I fell in love with the sport. My love for rowing was tested over the years, especially during the summer of '84, but it stayed intact.

While I was writing, Paul married a beautiful young woman, and now they have two boys. Harry Parker married the stroke of the '84 Olympic eight, and now they have a little girl. Tiff married his longtime girlfriend Kristy, and now they have a girl and a boy. Dan Louis also married, and they have a baby boy. Popular pastime, making babies.

In the spring of '86, I was invited to sail in the America's Cup, which put this story on hold. Following a long line of rowers-turned-sailors, I signed on as a *grinder*, the crewman who provides the muscle on board a 12-meter yacht. Spending a year before the mast, as the lowest man in our syndicate's hierarchy, put to rest any doubts I might have had regarding my ability to thrive in a team situation. My boat, the *USA* from San Francisco, performed well in Fremantle, but we were unable to stop the big man, Dennis Conner.

Jim Dietz became the head sculling coach for the U.S. team at the 1988 Seoul Olympics. For his quad, he selected John Strotbeck, Jack Frackleton, Gregg Montesi, and Charlie Altekruse. I attended the '88 Games as a journalist, but unfortunately I never saw the U.S. quad compete because I only visited the racecourse on the day of the finals.

Pam Cruz, my beautiful girlfriend, whose green-grey eyes pierced like diamonds, had her own story, and it was not about something as insignificant as rowing. Pam's story was about cancer. Pamela Ruth Cruz died on June 8, 1988. Only lately have I come to realize that a big part of me died with her. A very big part.

Finally, I returned to this story. I wrote another draft, then another, and finally this draft. Is it the last one? Yes, the story is now complete, except for one final image.

Winter, 1977-78, Diamond Bar, California. I was working on a 300-unit housing tract, trying to frame a 2,500-square foot roof - my first solo effort. A problem had come up. I'd spent a week trying to frame the garage, a portion of the roof that should have required only a few days. But I couldn't get it right. I was totally frustrated and ready to quit. My last hope was Carl Hilterbrand.

He drove up at 7:00 in the morning, as a hundred other carpenters were arriving for work.

After inspecting the garage, he said, "Your roof will have to come down, Brad. The ridge is too low. The guy who cut the rafters screwed you up, but you should've known better than to put them up without checking the length. The bottom line is you have to start over."

"Can't we jack it up, or something?" I asked. "It took me a week to get this far."

Without another word, Carl grabbed the hammer out of my nail bag and climbed onto the garage wall. Then he began swinging my hammer in huge arcs. I couldn't believe what I was seeing, nor could the other carpenters who had stopped to watch the action. With each swing of the hammer, a freeze block went sailing into the air. Splinters flew in every direction, as Carl turned my work into kindling. He busted-out every block and rafter and ridge, dismantling the garage roof in five minutes.

"Here's your hammer back," he said, after he climbed down. "Okay, listen. This is your first roof. I want you to remember two things: Do it right. Finish it. Very simple. Do it right. Finish it. If it takes you a month, then take a month. You can't quit, and you can't do it wrong. Get a payday out of this roof, or it'll haunt you until you die. Now you know: Do it right. Finish it."

Six years later I had occasion to see that roof three times a week, as Dan and I drove to Gilliam's Gym in West Covina. The house, poised along the 57 Freeway, looked fine, still upright, level ridge, no problems. I looked at it every time we passed.

The payday I had earned was spent long ago. More important, I had done it right, and I had finished it. The same is true for my life as a sculler. I'd done it right. I'd finished it.

The Puzzle is complete.

For photo captions, many more photos and contact
information, visit: www.bradalanlewis.com

CPSIA information can be obtained at www.ICGtesting.com
Printed in the USA
LVOW051920140812

294312LV00004B/39/P